REFUTING ISLAM

The Patriots Guide to Protecting America from Islam

REFUTING ISLAM

The Patriots Guide to Protecting America from Islam

by

Tom Wallace, Jr.

First Edition: November, 2015
Printed in the United States of America
Fundamental Publishers
ISBN-10: 1519417500
ISBN-13: 9781519417503

Table of Contents

Acknowledgement

We are all nothing without our gracious Lord and Savior Jesus Christ. I am thankful for a Father and Mother who taught me the fear of the LORD by word and deed.

Much praise should be given to my wife who has had to put up with my obsessive study of Islam and the trials we have endured on this journey. Her patience with my cantankerousness and her loyal support in what God has called me to do has been a tremendous blessing to me.

I must credit my family and father-in-law for the work they do for Fortress of Faith which allows me the time to study, preach, broadcast, and write this book. We all hope that this work will help the reader stand against an ideology that is committed to the destruction, not only of Christianity, but also governments who support liberty and democracy.

Preface

Islam has destroyed many nations and governments over a course of fourteen hundred years. America is vulnerable and will fall to Islam if we do not wake up to some sobering truths and change our course. We have been mishandling the issues of Islam, and this is putting our nation at great risk. If the bastion of freedom, the United States, falls who will carry the banner? Many of my Canadian friends have shared their fears with me and are worried about their future if America botches this threat from Islam.

For almost a decade, I have been arguing the issues of Islam. I have studied this religion in order to understand the source that drives fundamental Muslims to violence and terrorism. Having gained some valuable insights through my study, I have devised strategies that successfully win arguments on Islam. This book will give the reader real ammunition to effectively combat the issues of Islam in the arena of debate and argument.

The fix is not a top-down fix, but rather it is a bottom-up solution. Certainly, our government leaders need to learn the truths revealed in this book, but my goal is to teach laymen who will pressure and educate our Representatives on Capital Hill and our leaders in both the White House and the Pentagon. The battle for the truth about Islam needs to be won at the water cooler, at the dinner table, in the pulpits of America.

Rather than addressing the symptoms of the problem, I hope to get to the root. This book is not only designed to help Christian patriots to be informed on the issues but also to equip them with a winning strategy to rid our nation of the threat Islam poses.

In order to do this I have split this work into three parts. Please do not take the shortcut and jump to arguments and strategies. Each part builds upon the other. The first section not only addresses our mishandling of the issues but also contains important information about Islam and its strategy to destroy us. A successful general is not only going to be acquainted with the strengths of his army; but he will also acquaint himself with his enemy's strengths and strategies. The second part outlines the strategies we want to employ to achieve our aim. The final section contains the vast evidence we have available to prove our case that Islam is evil, destructive, and an enemy of the American way of life.

At the back of this book I have added a glossary of Islamic terms with a pronunciation guide to help with the pronunciation of difficult Arabic words. However, since the rules of translation from Arabic into English are somewhat loose, you may notice different spellings and pronunciations of these words. For example, is it Qur'an or is it Koran? Perhaps it's like the battle between British

English and American English, or maybe one version is more scholarly than the other. As I have been educated both in Britain and in America, I sometimes get confused as to who uses what spellings or pronunciations. The glossary is condensed but I believe it will be of help to you and you may want to refer to it often as you go through this book.

I have attempted to be brief and tackle the issues without filling this work with needless anecdote and stories. People read shorter books because they educate, hit their target, and set the reader on the path to action. You may find my writing style unorthodox and lacking in literary refinement. Perhaps you can forgive me for that if I achieve my goal: giving you tried and tested tools to oppose a destructive ideology that masquerades as a religion.

Part I: MISTAKES WE ARE MAKING

Chapter One

THE FANTACIZERS

Before we get stuck into this topic I need to make something clear. This book is not going to be about bashing Muslims. I hope that the reader will come to love Muslims as I do. However, this book will be making a critical analysis of the religion of Islam and its prophet Muhammad.

I imagine that many in North America would readily say that they view Islam as an enemy of their way of life. Yet there are many who are not convinced. Since many are sitting on the fence and afraid to form an opinion for or against the subject, it is treated as taboo.

We will address the militant, political, and cultural issues of Islam, but they are symptomatic issues, not the root problem. It is more productive for us dig into the ideology of Islam because this is the source. Once we have a firm grasp of the ideology of Islam, we will be on the right path to deal with it effectively.

PLAYING MAKE-BELIEVE

America is trying to live in a make-believe world. We live in fantasies that any logical thinker would reject. For example, Bruce Jenner says that he is a female trapped in a male's body. He now claims that he is a woman even though every natural chromosome in his body proves that he is a male. The fantasizers who celebrate his courage show their own foolishness. There was a time when this kind of nonsense would have been treated as a mental disorder.

America butchers unborn children while claiming that they are just removing superfluous tissue. Yet, a person is arrested and charged with double homicide if they are guilty of murdering a pregnant woman.

Professors tell us that, billions of years ago, nothing exploded from nothing which made everything and from it came perfectly shaped spheres which fell into a deliberate orbit. Then something crawled out of an organic soup and evolved into a highly sophisticated creature that over millions of years somehow became a human with a PhD.

Another fantasy is that some men are born to naturally love and marry another man. Anyone with an elementary knowledge of plumbing knows this is not possible. Males cannot procreate with males, and females cannot procreate with females. It is unnatural, and a logical minded person with no bias would readily come to this conclusion.

Now let's interject the issues of Islam into this nonsense. Since 1979 we have been attacked by Muslims in the name of Allah. The 'spin' doctors know how gullible Americans can be so they sell us the politically correct version that Islam is a religion of peace. These fantasizers believe that telling the lie long enough and loud enough will somehow make it true.

THE PC AGENDA

For many years I have said that political correctness will be the death of our nation. The PC agenda tries to control the talking points and shape the rhetoric so that they can sell their lies with some form of believability. The fantasy they are selling re-defines Islam by saying Muslims that perform terrorism are not real Muslims, rather they are *radical* Muslims. They demand that we accept the illusion that these *extremist, radical* Muslims are hijacking a peaceful religion. I'm afraid that the only thing they hijacked on 9/11 was airplanes. The Muslims who hijacked these planes and killed almost three thousand people on that fateful September morning were following the true teachings of their prophet Muhammad. They are not *radicals* perverting Islam, rather they are following the true doctrines of Islam.

Do you remember what happened to Bill O'Reilly on *The View*, October 2002? Thirteen months after the 9/11 attack, O'Reilly correctly said, "Muslims attacked us on 9/11." The guardians of the PC agenda, Whoopi Goldberg and Joy Behar, were livid. They stormed off the set fuming because O'Reilly did not describe the attackers as *radical* Muslims. They drove a message home: do not refer to Jihadists as Muslims. You must emphasize they are *radical* Muslims and not real Muslims.

Webster defines radical as something "very different from the usual" or something "very different from the traditional." When we use the term *radical*, we are saying that the actions of the *radical* Muslim are not normal for Islam; it is not the tradition. If you and I will not join their make-believe world, we will be treated as hateful, bigoted Islamophobes.

These fantasizers cannot tolerate anyone describing Muslims as murderers or saying Islam is evil. So the PC agenda has dreamed up new classifications. They are not Muslims; rather they are *Islamists*. These heinous acts do not describe Islam but *Islamism*. Fantasizers tell us that real Imams teach a peaceful Islam. This is the Kool-Aid they need us to drink to join their fantasy world. Sadly, the media has been drinking it by the gallon.

THE DANGER OF ISLAM

Like Christians, Muslims have a Great Commission in their scriptures. However, it is very different from the Christian Great Commission. Muhammad gave his final instructions before he died on his deathbed. We read it in the ninth chapter of the Qur'an:

> *Surah 9:29 "Fight those who believe not in Allah nor the Last Day, nor hold that forbidden which hath been forbidden by Allah and His Apostle, nor acknowledge the religion of Truth, (even if they are) of the People of the Book, until they pay the Jizya with willing submission, and feel themselves subdued."*

Muhammad was mildly partial to Christians. He believed that Christians were the closest to the faith and practice of Islam (Surah 5:82 *"you will certainly find the nearest in friendship to those who believe to be those who say: We are Christians"*).

However, when Muhammad was on his deathbed he then declared Christians as *mushrikūn* (polytheist), claiming that they were not true monotheist because they worship three Gods: God the Father, God the Son, and Mary (Muhammad's understanding of Christianity was seriously lacking).

In his last commandment Mohammad orders Muslims to fight any who do not submit to Muhammad's god, Allah, or anyone who rejects Muhammad as Allah's prophet, even if they be "people of the book [Bible]." Muslims are to do one of three things to unbelievers: convert them, enslave and force them to pay the Jizya, or kill them. [Note: I will explain the Jizya later on.]

Contrast this to the Christian Great Commission. Before Christ ascended into heaven he left his followers this command:

> *Matthew 28:19-20 "Go ye therefore, and teach all nations, baptizing them in the name of the Father, and of the Son, and of the Holy Ghost: Teaching them to observe all things whatsoever I have commanded you: and, lo, I am with you alway, even unto the end of the world. Amen."*

God prescribes this command for all Christians at all times to take the message of Christ to all people. It is to be done peacefully with preaching to persuade mankind to the truth. However, Islam prescribes for all Muslims at all times to take the sword of Allah to all *Kufr* (unbelievers). They make disciples by compulsion, shackle others into *Dhimmitude* (slavery), and kill those that remain.

The definition of Islam is not peace but rather surrender. The one who is surrendered is called a Muslim, which means the surrendered one. The idea is that the Muslim yields totally and surrenders to Allah. He is never allowed to doubt, question, or disobey. Islam dictates to the Muslim who and how he is to worship. It also dictates to him who and how he is to be governed. Muhammad was building more than just a religion; he was building an Empire. The Caliphate is the Emperor and supreme commander. We would describe this government as a dictatorship very similar to Nazism.

This ideology is in direct conflict with American values. We value freedom because of our Christian heritage: the freedom to choose our government, the freedom to choose whom we worship or if we worship at all. Our core values are a threat to the values of Islam. If Islam is to succeed, they must destroy freedom. This is one of the major reasons they hate us.

Equal Opportunity Destroyer

Islam wars not only with Christians but also with anything and anyone that does not submit and surrender to Muhammad's god, Allah. Dr. Bill Warner, the founder of *Political Islam.com* has carefully studied Islam for over forty years and has diligently researched the atrocities of Muslims over their fourteen hundred-year history. He calls it the *Tears of Jihad.*

A question we must start asking is how nations became Islamic. Syria for example, how did she become a Muslim State? Syria used to be a strong Christian nation. The first translation of the New Testament into a foreign language was Syriac for the Syrians. The great Church in Antioch that commissioned the great missionary and apostle, Paul, was located in Syria. In Acts 11:26 we find the disciples were called Christians first in Antioch, which was in Syria.

TEARS OF Jihad

- Africans   120 Million
- Christians 60 Million
- Hindus   80 Million
- Buddhist 10 Million
- Jews   100's of Thousands

Source: www.PoliticalIslam.com

It became Islamic as the second Caliph, Umar, came in with the sword and moved his Caliphate from Mecca to Damascus in Syria. He gave the Christian population three options: convert, death, or *dhimmitude* (slavery). By the way, this is exactly what Al-Baghdadi, the self-declared Caliph, and his ISIS army has been doing with the Christians in Syria. They identify the Christians as the followers

9

of the Nazarene (Jesus), and they spray paint the Arabic letter ن (N) on their houses, businesses, and churches. Today, ISIS offers the Christians in Syria the same options Umar gave: convert, death, or *dhimmitude.*

Jihadist groups like ISIS, Al Qaeda, Hammas, and Hezbollah, to name a few, are showing us the real face of Islam. The self-declared Caliph, Al Baghdadi, correctly said, "O Muslims, Islam was never for a day of the religion of peace. Islam is the religion of war. Your prophet was dispatched with a sword . . . . 'I came to you with slaughter'."[1]

Muhammad motivated his followers to fight for him with promises that would be appealing to young men. He promised them eternal rewards if they died in battle. These are called the seven blessings of the *Shahid* (pronounced *sha-heed* meaning martyr):

1. He is forgiven from the moment his blood is first shed.

2. He will be shown his place in Paradise.

3. He will be spared the trial of the grave.

4. He will be secure on the Day of Judgment.

5. Upon his head will be placed a crown of dignity, one ruby of which is better than this world and all that is in it.

6. He will be married to seventy-two virgins, and he will be able to ravage them through all eternity.

7. He will be permitted to intercede for seventy of his relatives.[2]

I was debating a Muslim on the topic of the seventy-two virgins. He said that the Arabic *Al-hoor aliyn* (virgins) could be translated raisins. I paused and said contemptuously, "Let's see if I understand this. So imagine I heard Muhammad promise to me that if I gave up my life in battle for Muhammad I would be eternally rewarded with the promise of—seventy-two raisins? (I hope they are chocolate covered raisins.) Do you seriously want me to buy that? Have you not also read all the sexual acts that the *Shahid* will do to these *raisins*?" He wanted to move to another subject.

By the way, you will not find the teaching of the seventy-two virgins in the Qur'an; it is in the Sunnah. The Qur'an are the words of the god Allah. The Sunnah are the words and deeds of the Prophet Muhammad. Muslims consider both works as scripture, and from them Muslims extrapolate their doctrines and laws, called the Sharia.

There has been much talk about the seventy-two virgins, which is the sixth blessing, but I want to draw your attention to the seventh blessing of the *Shahid*: the promise to plead for seventy family members. Women don't have much chance to get to heaven. Muhammad said that the vast majority of Hell is filled with women because they are deficient in mind[3] (I wonder how the feminists in America feel about that). It seems the greatest hope that a women has to get to heaven is if someone will plead to Allah for them.

11

Perhaps this is why many Muslim women in the Middle East, namely Israel, will pick one of their young children and will say to him every day, *'Yousef, you will be the one who gets to have the honor of bringing salvation to your family. You get to be the blessed one who will receive Allah's greatest reward. To be our Shahid, to have the greatest honor, our Mujahideen.'* That child will be raised to hate Jews and taught that the Jews have stolen the land that was the birthright of the Arabs through Ishmael. When Yousef grows up he will strap on a suicide vest and blow himself up in Jerusalem killing Jews and himself. That day his picture will be displayed around the community, and he will be honored as a hero. His mother will also celebrate and dance in the streets because she believes that she now has a place in heaven, for surely her son will plead for his mother.

A MISTAKE WE CAN'T AFFORD

We all make mistakes. The person who put the backspace key on the keyboard knew what he was doing. Some mistakes, we can look back and laugh at ourselves. However, some mistakes are too costly and disastrous. Europe made serious mistakes in dealing with Hitler. I am sure many would agree that if they acted sooner in dealing with the bully, millions of lives would not have perished in World War II.

America elected Obama, which has proven to be a huge mistake: a mistake that may cost us dearly. He refuses to address Islam head on. Islam declared war on us fourteen hundred years ago but we refuse to see Islam as an enemy. Pretending Islam is not at war with us is a mistake we cannot afford to make.

On July 6, 2015, President Obama held a press conference at the Pentagon to brief America on his handling of the war with ISIS. He said, "We will never be at war with Islam." He has said this a number of times, and even former President Bush communicated that our war is not with Islam but rather terrorism. We will never be safe if we fail to admit the truth and accept Islam as our enemy. Obama also showed the depth of his foolishness at the same press conference. He said, "ideologies are not defeated with guns but better ideas." [4]

In February of 2015, Marie Harf, State Department spokesperson for John Kerry, showed equal folly and said the US cannot "kill our way out" of the war with ISIS. "We need . . . . to go after the root causes that lead people to join these groups, whether it's lack of opportunity for jobs" [5] (No wonder our enemies are laughing at us). And let's not forget the biggest laugh when President Obama told the cadets at the Coast-Guard Academy in New London, Connecticut that America's biggest security threat is Global Warming. [6]

Obama claims to be an educated man but he lacks knowledge of history, and he also lacks common sense. This is personal to me, and it should be to the reader too. Obama is gambling our lives on his hope that we can defeat ISIS with better ideologies. It is a crying shame that we do not have a Press to challenge him on this foolish notion.

Questions like, "Mr. President, what are the better ideas? Please be specific." "Mr. President, where in history has this worked?"

Chapter Two

THE APPEASERS

PRIME MINISTER NEVILLE CHAMBERLAIN

America is making the same foolish mistakes that were made in the late 1930's. The Allied forces had no appetite for another world war. The West tried to make-believe that Hitler was not going to be a problem. Instead of acting with swift force when Germany broke the Treaty of Versailles the allies looked the other way. They did not act when Hitler started stockpiling weapons in 1935, a clear violation of the treaty.   Then Hitler moved his troops over the Rhineland, and again the Allies did nothing. When Hitler moved his troops into Austria, British Prime Minister Neville Chamberlain sought a peaceful solution.

A new pact was signed in Munich on September 30, 1938, thus giving Czechoslovakia, Slovakia, and parts of Ukraine to Hitler with the promise that he would not invade Poland. Chamberlain proudly waved the paper with Hitler's signature declaring peace in our time: hoping to appease a bully by giving in to his demands. It did not work then and it will not work today.

There are many, many similarities between Islam and Nazism. Both preach a supremacy doctrine. Both desire World domination and rule by a dictatorship. Both kill their dissidents, and both desire the destruction of the Jewish people.

The appeaser is working from a weak position. The appeaser is afraid to fight, and the bully sees weakness. The appeaser thinks he is getting peace by making concessions to the bully, but all it is doing is allowing the bully the time to build up enough strength to take the appeaser out.

SHARIAH COURTS IN THE UK

For a decade, I remember hearing Muslims say that Sharia law is coming to England. I dismissed it as dreamy thinking by the Muslims. I thought it would be impossible for that to occur, but I was wrong. I did not understand the agenda back then, but I certainly do now. I will never forget the day, September 14, 2008. It was the London Sunday Times newspaper that announced that Sharia Law courts were opening with the governments backing. In order to keep peace with Muslims in Britain, the Brits appeased them by adding Sharia to the British legal code. At first, there were only seven Sharia courts[7], but in less than twelve months there were already eighty-five Sharia law courts opened.[8]

These courts are limited to civil, family law issues for now, but if the status quo remains the same, the courts will likely be enlarged to allow criminal cases also. Now this does not mean that all of England is under Sharia law. But what it does mean is that England—perhaps the third or forth most powerful nation on Earth—declared that they are a sovereign nation that subjects everyone living on their Island to its laws *except the Muslims*. They get a pass. They don't have to live by British law like everyone else; they can choose to be governed by their own laws.

Needless to say, this is dangerous—and can I say just plain stupid! Why in the world would England do such a foolish thing you ask? They did it to appease Muslims. Everyone knows what happens if you don't give into the demands of Muslims. They riot, burn, kill, and create mayhem. England allowed too many Muslims to immigrate into their country, and due to their numbers Arch Bishop of Canterbury, Rowan Williams, said Sharia law courts in Britain were "unavoidable."[9] Seven months later the government bowed to Muslim demands and surrendered their sovereignty to a tyrannical ideology. Just seventy years after the Munich pact to appease the bullies of Nazism, Britain attempted to appease a different group of bullies, those from Islam.

America is also following the wrong path. When America is weak, the bullies of the world see their opportunity to knock us down. In the 70's, with Jimmy Carter at the helm, Iran saw our weakness and assaulted our Embassy, holding 52 US diplomats hostage for 444 days. Then America elected a strong leader who refused to appease the enemy. Iran released our American staff the day Ronald Reagan took office.

BARBARY PIRATE WARS

America tried to appease Muslims in the past, but it did not work then either. A valuable lesson of our history is being lost in the schools of America. As our young nation was recovering from our battle for independence, we set out to trade goods with the world. As our merchant ships got around the coast of North Africa, the Muslim pirates would seize our vessels and hold both ship and crew for ransom.

This was a major headache for the United States' second President, John Adams. We had a sizable land army but hardly a navy. The Marine Corp was inaugurated, but the defense budget was insufficient to build our military. Adams and Congress felt our only option was to appease the Muslims and pay the ransom demands. But what does this teach a bully? They learn that if they seize our vessels and demand money, America will pay, so they kept doing it. This was the wrong move and it was bankrupting America's Treasury.

In March of 1785, Thomas Jefferson, diplomatic commissioner, met with the Algerian Ambassador, Abd Al-Rahman, in London to try to understand why Algeirs declared war on America as we had shown them no aggression. The Library of Congress will likely have Jefferson's letter that he wrote to Congress explaining the Algerian's reasons. Al-Rahman said,

> *"It was written in the Koran, that all nations who should not have acknowledged their authority were sinners, that it was their right and duty to make war upon whoever they could find and to make slaves of all they could take as prisoners, and that every Mussulman who*

should be slain in battle was sure to go to Paradise."[10]

Adams tried to find a peaceful solution with the Muslims of Algeria, Morocco, Libya, and Tunis. The US made many treaties with them, but the Muslims broke each one. Later in this book we will discuss why Muslims are obligated to deceive the enemy. After all, Muhammad said many times, "war is deceit." You will find later in this book that treaties with the *Kufr* means nothing to Muslims.

Appeasement only delays the inevitable: war. Appeasing only buys us a false hope that we have averted war. Meanwhile, it gives the bully time to build their army and accumulate weapons.

Thomas Jefferson purchased a two volume English translation of the Qur'an while in London. He studied it to see for himself why these Muhammadans were violent. This led him to act differently than Adams when he became America's third President. He returned their aggression with aggression. He was famous for coining the phrase, "not one penny for tribute but millions for defense."

Jefferson also built our Navy and Marine Corps and sent them to fight the Muslims from 1801-1815. The hymn of the Marines references this Barbary War with the Muslims, *"from the halls of Montezuma to the shores of Tripoli."* This is the Tripoli in Libya, North Africa. The US Naval ships that fought in the two Barbary Wars were:

USS Intrepid, USS Philadelphia, USS Enterprise, USS President, USS Constitution, USS Constellation, USS Congress, USS Chesapeake, USS United States, USS Erie, USS Ontario, and the USS John Adams.

It is fitting to bring to remembrance the great wisdom of that British statesman, Edmund Burke. He said, "All that is necessary for the triumph of evil is for good men to do nothing." The appeaser is a coward. Cowards wish for peace but do nothing. Doing nothing brings the coward and his family death. History bears this to be true.

Chapter Three

THE REFORMERS

Another mistake we are making is to think that Islam can be reformed. Some Muslims are trying to reform Islam to make it a kinder, gentler religion. These reformers are sending confusing messages to America and are making the situation worse, not better. Let me explain.

The reformer is inventing a god of their own imagination. They don't like a judgmental Allah or a religion of war and hate. They desire peace and a live-and-let-live approach to life. These Muslims have heard that Christianity had a reformation, so why can't they.

They have no idea what the real Christian reformation was about. They just know that the Inquisition was full of bloodshed by some Christian groups and the reformers took a violent Christian religion and made it peaceful. They think this is what Islam needs.

The problem is that the Christian Reformation was taking a perversion of Christianity that had slipped away from Christ's design back to the fundamentals, back to the Bible. The Muslim Reformers of Islam today are actually doing the opposite. They are rejecting the orthodox, fundamental teachings of Muhammad and changing them to something opposite from what Muhammad taught. They willfully ignore the militant passages and interpret them away while clinging solely to the earlier passages of the Qur'an that were peaceful in nature.

We should note that there are some Christians trying to do that with the Bible and with Jehovah God. Some say, "My god does not condemn homosexuals. My god is not judgmental." When they do that, they are breaking the second commandment by making up a god of their own imagination.

Some of the popular Muslim reformers in America that we see on the media outlets are:

Harris Zafar - A young, dashing, eloquent Muslim who lives in Portland, Oregon. He is the US spokesperson for Ahmadiyya Muslim Community. They are considered a cult in the orthodox Islamic world. Their headquarters are in England, and their founder claimed in 1889 to be Jesus of Nazareth (Muslims are also waiting for the coming of Jesus).

Dr. Zuhdi Jasser MD - Another Muslim reformer we see a lot on TV. He is a former US Naval Officer and the founder of the American Islamic Forum for Democracy. He is a strong advocate for the US Constitution and Democracy.

Ayaan Hirsi Ali - Now a US citizen, she was born in Somalia, reared in the Netherlands, and wed to a Scottish historian and commentator. Ayaan has been listed by Times magazine as one of the hundred most influential people in the world. It is not clear if Ayaan has renounced Islam and is no longer a Muslim but she lives in hiding for exposing Islam's crimes against women. It is clear that she believes Islam should be reformed. Her latest book *Heretic* has the subtitle *Why Islam Needs a Reformation Now.*

These reformers are also trying to live in a fantasy that Islam can be a religion of peace. One big problem is that American leaders get to know these people and they find them genuinely believing Islam to be religion of peace. These American leaders take their word for it and join this fantasy about Islam because, if it could be true, Islam would be palatable to America. The problem is that these leaders have not done their due diligence to study the scriptures of Islam for themselves to get to the truth.

A recent example of such a leader is Governor Bobby Jendal. I like him and what he has done for the State of Louisiana, but he is wrong about the solution for homegrown terrorism. A day after Muhammad Yousef Abdulazeez, a twenty-four year old Muslim, shot and killed four Marines and one Sailor in Chattanooga, Tennessee, Governor Jendal said on the Kelly File,

> *"Until [Imams] make clear that within Islam it is not acceptable for these murderers to feel like they're going to be martyrs and they need to make clear, they are not going to be rewarded in the afterlife rather they're going straight to hell where they belong"[11]*

It would be nice if the Imams of Islam would all preach this message, but it is a perversion of Islam. It is not what

Muhammad preached, and it is not what Allah gave to Muhammad.

As a person of faith, I believe in an almighty God: a God who created and gave life to man and communicates His will and message to mankind through His Holy Book. Who is man to alter the message given by God? I would scoff at anyone who demands preachers of America to change the message of God from the Bible to fit some politician's agenda.

You and I don't see the Qur'an as God's revelation, but Muslims do. Orthodox Muslims see these reformers as heretics, blasphemers, and in danger of Allah's wrath for changing the words of Mohammad and Allah. They scoff at those who preach something contrary to what their prophet gave them. Such preaching is not fruitful nor does it have any chance of persuading the fundamentalists of Islam.

Another problem that these reformers create is that it gives Jihadists a place to hide and conceal their identity. The Jihadists now have a place to hide in front of us. They spout off publicly that they love America, freedom, and democracy, as this is acceptable to Americans. They declare that Islam is a religion of peace but they know they are deceiving us. They are wolves in the sheep's clothing of reformed Islam. Cloaked as a reformer, they covertly carry out their sedition to destroy America from within. This is exactly what the Muslim Brotherhood Memorandum prescribed.

In 2004, the FBI raided the home of Ismail Embrasse, A.K.A. Abdul Hassan. In a secret room hidden in his basement, they found a cache of documents, videos, and computer files. The prize document was the Memorandum to the affiliate groups in North America. It outlined their strategies, and on page seven it declared,

> *"The process of settlement is a Civilization-Jihadist Process with all the word means. The Ikhwan [Muslim Brotherhood] must understand that their work in America is a kind of grand jihad in eliminating and destroying the Western civilization from within and sabotaging its miserable house by their hands and the hands of the believers."*[12]

PART II : METHODS TO EMPLOY

CHAPTER FOUR

TAKING A STAND

The LORD has blessed our radio ministry. Our program has grown from one station broadcasting over 1.5 million people to 250 stations broadcasting over 40 million people in four years. I reached syndication on a National radio Network in less than two years. It is not because I am a talented businessman and a great communicator. Rather it is because North America is hungry for the truth and when you give people the truth and deliver it in the correct manner, they respond positively.

Let's face it, what main stream media and the government are selling about Islam does not pass the sniff test.

We admire those who throw off the PC shackles and tell it like it is. I believe this is why America has been enamored by Donald Trump's presidential bid. It shows us how much hate we have in our hearts for the professional politician who parses every word so carefully and dances around the issues to please everybody and offend nobody (if that's possible).

Claiming 'I'm offended', is a strategy liberals use as a weapon. Liberals don't usually have good arguments, so, when they don't have substance to win the arguments, they attack their opponents by labeling them or playing the victim and portraying their opponents as tyrants. Their favorites are calling us 'Offensive' 'Intolerant' 'Hateful' 'Bigot' 'Racist' etc. Then they suggest the patriot has a mental illness to hold the views they hold and say you have a phobia. They diagnose you in the court of public opinion as a 'fill-in-the-blank-o-phobia' (Homophobia, Islamophopia, Xenophobia, Afrophobia etc.)

Let's briefly address the fallacy of the label 'Intolerant'. Suppose you get called intolerant, you might feel low because you fear that your peers and friends will see you as narrow-minded, bigoted and downright rude. Stop and think this through, isn't the person who labeled you as intolerant being intolerant too? They are being narrow-minded and not allowing you the freedom to speak your views and hoping that now that you are *labeled*, you will just shut up. Liberals are the most intolerant people I know. Yet they are the ones calling everyone else intolerant. You should point out to them their hypocrisy. We should also note that Muslims are learning and using these tactics too.

Another point you should make on this issue, being intolerant can be good. Being intolerant could mean that you are discerning. Would you tolerate lies, theft, and murder? There are some things in this world we should not tolerate. Thank God for some intolerant people like Winston Churchill. Because of him, the Allies of World War II did not tolerate the bully Hitler. They were resolved to not tolerate Nazism, and because they took a stand to defeat it you and I were able to grow up in a democratic republic and not a dictatorship.

A CULTURE OF COWARDS

America has been developing a culture of cowards. Everyone is afraid that they might offend someone and be *labeled*. We have become soft and non-offensive, retreating to the safe havens of our homes letting the liberals and the godless, systematically destroy our Nation and values. We have become professional moaners and groaners about the tragedies that have befallen our Nation, but we are too cowardly to do anything about it. We keep saying, "That's terrible, someone should do something about it", yet we do nothing and hope that God will just rapture us out of this mess so that we don't have to address the problem. I believe in the imminent return of Christ, it could be today, but if it is not for another generation or two, what are we leaving for our kids and grandkids if we sit on our hands doing nothing about the problem? They will inherit a mess that we could have adverted <u>if only</u> we would have taken a stand.

Today, for the most part, we have cowards in the pulpits of America. The American Culture and Faith Institute commissioned Barna Research to conduct a study for them. Their two year study was released in August of 2014 which exposed a dirty secret about American Pastors. Barna polled thousands of preachers from multiple denominations and asked them, 'Does the Bible speak to the controversial political issues of our day, things like abortion, homosexuality etc.?' Nine out of Ten Pastors replied, Yes! Then they were asked, do you preach about those things in your pulpit. Sadly the result was only one out of ten. This is disgraceful and indefensible.

Reasons Why Pastors will not preach about the Controversial Political Issues

- 32% Fear threat of punishment by IRS / ACLU
- 23% Believe Politics and Church are separate
- 16% Pressure from deacon / elder
- 13% Denominational constraints
- 9% Personal distaste for Politics
- 8% Unfamiliar about the issues

Source: Barna Reasearch Aug. 2014

When you analyze the reasons why pastors will not address the issues from their pulpits, it reveals that one quarter are just ignorant to what the separation of church and state is really about. Separation of church and state was not to keep Christians out of government affairs; but rather it was designed to keep the government out of the affairs of our churches.

When you boil the reasons down to their bare essence, we find that preachers fear man more than they fear God. Almost two-thirds of the pastors were afraid of either the IRS, deacons in their church, or denominational condemnation.

Please allow me a brief detour while I get on my rant for a moment. There is a lot of confusion and misunderstanding about what pastors can and cannot do in politics and the IRS code, so let's get it straight. When Lyndon Johnson was running for re-election for US Senate, preachers and some non-profit groups became problematic to his campaign. The 83rd Congress was just about to vote a tax reform bill (P.L. 83-591) which was the first overhaul of the IRS tax code since its inception in 1913. Senator Johnson slipped an amendment (known as the Johnson amendment) into the bill prohibiting non-profits 501 (c) 3 types (which include registered churches) from endorsing a political candidate or raising funds to support a political candidate.

The bill passed on July 2nd, 1954. For 166 years, preachers openly participated in politics from their pulpits and publicly endorsed God fearing political candidates before their congregations as the Constitution allows. The Johnson Amendment is illegal and will not stand up in court.

I encourage every pastor to participate in *Pulpit Freedom Sunday.* It is a movement of patriotic pastors who exercise their constitutionally protected freedom to speak truth in all areas of life from the pulpit. This is an initiative of the *Alliance Defending Freedom.* They hope to go to court in order to have the Johnson Amendment struck down as unconstitutional for its regulation of sermons, which is protected by the first amendment.

A growing number of pastors are courageously endorsing political candidates from their pulpits. Not only are they endorsing candidates during their sermons, but they also publish transcripts of the sermons and send them to the IRS. In the year 2014, almost two thousand churches did this, and their churches are proudly listed on the ADF website. [13]

At the very least, Pastors need to follow the advice of my friend Attorney David Gibbs III, founder of the National Center for Life and Liberty. He says that Pastors can endorse political candidates as long as they do not use the Church's "dime or time." Rather than using church resources to tell your congregation who you endorse, write your endorsement from your own computer, using your own paper and stamps. From the pulpit, you can certainly preach on the moral issues. You can urge your congregation to vote on Christian morals, and name the candidates who stand against abortion, same-sex marriage, etc.

According to the *Pew Initiative*, our Churches can change the face of politics in America if the amount of Christian voters would increase only increase by 10%. If Christians are not going to pick our elected officials, then non-Christians will pick them for us. The Pew Initiative reports that on average, 25-50% of most congregations are not even registered to vote. Of those who are registered to vote, 40% (4 out 10) did not vote in the last Presidential election. In General elections, only 25% of the congregation will vote. We complain that we do not have good candidates to vote for and we are tired of voting for the lessor of the two evils so 75% of our registered voters don't even bother to vote. The primaries are where we have a good chance of voting in good candidates who are trying to get on the ticket, but sadly, only 5% of registered voters in churches will even vote in the primaries. This is shameful!!! Did you know that most candidates are determined by only 1-3% of the votes?

Pastors can find out who is registered and not registered to vote in their church at PewVote.com. It is free and confidential. The Family Research Council has a wonderful program helping churches to hold voter registration drives. They will walk you through the process, step by step.

Now let's return from the detour. Perhaps the reason we have cowards in the pulpits is because we have cowards in the pews. Carnal congregations look for carnal shepherds who will not nip at their heels on the issues of sin. The Apostle Paul warned Timothy of this, "For the time will come when they will not endure sound doctrine; but after their own lusts shall they heap to themselves teachers, having itching ears."

If your pastor is a coward who is too afraid to preach against the controversial sins and if your church refuses to support or encourage him in taking a stand for righteousness, then let me give you some friendly advice. Leave! Pray for the church, but search for a good Bible-preaching church which has a pastor who will preach the whole counsel of God's Word. If you try to change them you will be seen as one sowing seeds of discord among the brethren.

If you have a pastor who is among the one-out-of-ten who is not afraid to speak up, cherish and encourage him. Remember, he is a man, and capable of buckling under pressure. However, if he knows that the congregation has his back and will support him even when times get tough, he will lead. These men are rare and need our support, so help them by making sure they know you are standing with them.

SALT AND LIGHT

We have failed in being the *salt and light* that God commanded us to be. We are in trouble because we as Christians have not done our duty.

For most Christians, the meaning of *salt and light* is just evangelizing the lost. This is a major part but not the sole part. Salt preserves and purifies. Light reveals and exposes things. God calls upon Christians not only to live His standards but also to proclaim them. When evil shows up in our community, God's people are to speak out against it. We are to identify what is evil, lewd, wicked, and publicly protest it. This is being *salt and light*.

We were sold a false bill of goods in the 60's and 70's, Christians were told that they are not to be involved in politics. Separation of church and state was turned upside down in the courts, and since that time Christians retreated to the shadows. Who do you think benefits when Christians are not involved in politics? Godless men and women benefit and they sweep in to fill the void. They get elected to the halls of legislation and pass unrighteous laws. If

Christians step down, then the ungodly become our judges, governors, and presidents.

Charles Finney delivered a powerful sermon in New York on December 4, 1873. Wrapping up his sermon entitled "The Decay of Conscience," Finney concluded,

> *"Brethren, our preaching will bear its legitimate fruits. If immorality prevails in the land, the fault is ours in a great degree. If there is a decay of conscience, the pulpit is responsible for it. If the public press lacks moral discrimination, the pulpit is responsible for it. If the church is degenerate and worldly, the pulpit is responsible for it. If the world loses its interest in religion, the pulpit is responsible for it. If Satan rules in our halls of legislation, the pulpit is responsible for it. If our politics become so corrupt that the very foundations of our government are ready to fall away, the pulpit is responsible for it."[14]*

I am convinced that it is not too late to rise up and take our country back if we choose to stand and do our duty. We have to choose a new normal and abandon the current approach and way of thinking. Let's admit we are at fault for not doing our duty, but then look forward and upward. We can do it; there are good options ahead for us. First, we have to change our thinking and approach to the issues at hand. Then we need to change the thinking of others. We can win the arguments, change despondent hearts and even alter our nation's direction back to righteousness.

Now let's start addressing the issue of Islam and get to a winning strategy. I am going to focus on the practical aspects of this task and hope the reader understands that we cannot succeed in anything without God. So let's not forget the spiritual element to this task.

The next five chapters will outline steps that form five important principles that will place you in an advantaged position. Just as armies want to position themselves strategically for the battle we want to be positioned on the high ground.

CHAPTER FIVE

SPEAK THE TRUTH IN LOVE

I believe there are three arenas in which Islam can be defeated in North America: the arena of the Muslim mind, the arena of the skeptic's mind, and the arena of our legal system. To have victory in these arenas, we need to form the right arguments and teach these truths to our fellow patriots so we can all join together in the struggle against Islam.

Someone once said it is not important whether you win or lose but how you play the game. I believe we can both win and play well, and it is my aim to teach you how.

The old adage that you can catch more flies with honey than with vinegar has been around for centuries because there is truth to the statement. If you are trying to win a person to your view, don't be caustic in your arguments and actions. My dad taught me early in life, you are seldom persuasive when you are abrasive. This nugget of wisdom has served me well, and it will reap benefits to you also if you employ it.

I greatly admire two men who patterned this standard and accomplished the impossible with it: Mahatma Gandhi and Martin Luther King Jr. Gandhi's short stature of five foot, three inches cast a giant shadow over the nation of India.

Born in the lowly caste system of India, he improved his condition by educating himself as a lawyer in England. His tenacious resolve coupled with his peaceful, gentle spirit brought about India's independence from the shackles of the British Empire. It is a shame America is largely ignorant of what this man accomplished and the manner in which he performed it. Not only did he cause the British Empire to crumble and leave India but he also healed the rift between the Muslims and the Hindus in his nation—no small task I might add.

Like Gandhi, Martin Luther King modeled a peaceful but persistent leadership using compassionate, logical appeals to fight for equal rights. Both of these men changed their world without war and without hate-filled language.

I understand the passion and even hate that Americans have towards Islam and Muslims because we were deliberately and willfully attacked without provocation on our part. Jihadis continue to hurl threats at us, and one can be justified to be filled with indignation over this. It is tempting to give into the lust of the flesh and jump into the gutter to vent our frustrations, however, our cause is better served by taking the higher moral ground. This takes discipline and wisdom.

We could say that Gandhi and King learned their technique from the master, Jesus Christ. Jesus of Nazareth did not rule as a king over a kingdom and he never commanded an army. Instead, the master teacher taught us in word and in deed that the pen is mightier than the sword. Christ gave us

41

a book, not a sword. In fact, He told us those who live by the sword will die by the sword. His doctrine was boldly spread by His disciples from house to house. By chapter five in the book of Acts, His doctrine filled all of Jerusalem, and by chapter seventeen His doctrine had turned the world upside down. Truth shared with bold compassion is contagious.

You can have the truth, but if you peddle it with immoral methods, it extinguishes the potency and validity of the message. The pragmatist who believes the end justifies the means is often an immoral man. He will abandon values and employ evil methods if he is consumed with reaching his goal. America celebrates and rewards winners. This brings temptation to abandon standards. For example, seven-time Tour de France winner Lance Armstrong cheated using performance-enhancing drugs. My point is to join the resistance against Islam, but let's be ladies and gentlemen, and let's fight the fight with honesty and dignity.

I mentioned two good examples we should follow. Here are two examples not to follow. Each of these men, no doubt feel justified for their actions, but their methods were destructive and counterproductive. The first is Pastor Terry Jones from Gainesville, Florida. He caught national attention by threatening to burn the Qur'an on September 11, 2010. His rhetoric was bold but lacked compassion and was filled with offense. He became incendiary on the issues of Islam and later carried out his threat and publicly burned the Qur'an twice.

Jones earned the bigot label which will stick with him because he proved himself to be a bigot, and he lost credibility with the public at large because of his offensive tactics. Now when he was arrested in Dearborn, Michigan I did support his rights to free speech. The first amendment gives rights to all speech, even offensive speech. What Jones said about Islam is largely true but he turned people off because his message was delivered with hate and offense.

The second example is another preacher, Reuben Israel. In 2011 and 2012 he came with his buddies to the Arab Festival in Dearborn, Michigan. What their signs said was true but offensive to Muslims. "Muhammad is a Pedophile," "Your religion will send you to Hell," etc.

I was in Dearborn in 2011 when the police had a "free speech zone," and they kept the Christian antagonists like Reuben's bunch at the edge of the festival and there was a large presence of law enforcement. They riled up the Muslims, and I saw Muslims throw plastic water bottles at the protesters. The free speech zone provided enough distance to keep the hostilities to a minimum.

However, in 2012 the organizers made a mistake and removed the free speech zone which allowed the antagonists to walk freely into the festival. Not only did they show up with their signs, but they came with a pig's head stuck on a spike. The whole purpose was to protest, offend, and incite Muslims to anger. Swine are *haram*, forbidden in Islam, and I imagine you would get an angry response from Orthodox Jews if some showed up with a pig's head at a Jewish street festival. I suspect you would also get an angry response if someone showed up at a Christian street festival with an effigy of Christ hanging in a pool of urine, or someone burning the Holy Bible.

I have been going to the festival for a number of years to help local ministries evangelize the Muslims. The festival provided great opportunities to witness to one hundred thousand Muslims. Reuben's group, and the like, harmed the efforts of the local missionaries and pastors who paid to have booths at the festival.

In 2012, I witnessed the law enforcement tell Reuben that they are not going to hang around and protect them, that they were on their own. When the deputies withdrew, the Muslim youth started throwing plastic water bottles, milk crates, and stones at these "Christians".

I witnessed three waves of assaults by the Muslim youth on Reuben's group. After the first skirmish I slipped into Reuben's group to interview him. I began quoting some Bible verses to him, II Cor. 6:3, "Give no offense that the ministry be not blamed." Eph. 4:15 "Speak the truth in love." Rom. 14:16 "Let not your good be evil spoken of."

I asked, "How is the message on your signs and the pig's head speaking the truth in love?" He justified his offense by citing John the Baptist who went to Herod and spoke painfully to Herod of his adultery. We had to cut the interview off as another wave of attacks by the Muslim youth began, and I retreated to safety.

The Monday after the event, I wrote on my blog that there were two winners and two losers in Dearborn, Michigan over the weekend. One winner was some Muslims who got to go home with pride because they defended their prophet's honor. Another winner was some Christians because they got to fly home saying they suffered for Jesus at the hand of violent Muslims. However, there were two losers that day. The City of Dearborn got another bloody nose over the headlines of Muslims behaving badly. The other loser in the event was Jehovah God because He was not honored by what His followers did in inciting the conflict. The methods and message used in both of these examples harmed our cause rather than helping it.

We sometimes struggle to communicate the message properly. Two preachers were standing on the road side, each holding signs to warn drivers as they passed by. One sign said, "The End is Near!" The other sign said "Turn or Burn!" Both spoke the truth but neither communicated the warning very well. The danger would have been communicated better if it said, "Bridge Out".

We can do better! Speaking the truth in Love is essential. Now let's move onto the next important step.

CHAPTER SIX

DIVIDE AND CONQUER

The next step has two parts to it.

PART ONE: DIVIDE THE PEOPLE FROM THE RELIGION

The people are the Muslims. The religion is Islam. The word Muslim means the submitted one. Islam means submit, surrender. This may not seem significant, but it is important to divide the people from the religion when you are refuting Islam. If you don't, you will be seen as attacking people and this will get you into a heap of trouble. You may recall that I started chapter one with this clarification. We are not attacking persons; we are addressing issues of a religion.

MAKING OBJECTIVE ARGUMENTS

Separating the people from the religion gives you the higher ground from which to form objective arguments. Subjective arguments are faulty if your subject is a person. The person may not be a good model of their faith. If the person lacks knowledge, dedication, and practice of their faith, then your argument will be shot down quickly.

I hate it when someone rejects Christ because of the poor testimony of a failing Christian. In return, we cannot judge Islam because of a particular Muslim who may not be fully following what Islam teaches. We must separate the people from the religion because they may be a poor example of the believers and may provide weak evidence on which to build a case.

Once we have set aside the emotion and the issues of the Muslim people, we gain leverage using the doctrines of the religion of Islam. This is being objective in our approach. Let's take an objective look at Islam. Islam has simply two things we can be very objective about, its prophet and its scriptures. Muhammad is dead and so are his companions. We can look at their teachings and the actions of the followers of its fourteen hundred year history. The Qur'an and the Sunnah make up their scriptures, which have no life, no voice, no emotion, just simply words on a page to be examined and analyzed.

LIBEL AND SLANDER

Libel vs. Slander

Libel and slander are types of defamatory statements.

Libel is a written defamatory statement.

Slander is a spoken or oral defamatory statement.

Source: www.nolo.com

Separating the people from the Religion has another benefit: it will keep you out of legal trouble. You can find yourself in a world of trouble if you are guilty of libel or slander. For the moment, it is not against the law in America to denigrate the religion of Islam but there are efforts to change that. Our neighbors in Canada are finding that they are not free to speak out against Islam, even if what they say is true. There are hate speech laws instituted in Canada much like those of some European countries. The Human Rights Commission sued Journalist Ezra Levant because a Muslim said he was offended at something Ezra Levant said about Islam. I have had Ezra on my show a couple of times and he told us that he spent over $100,000 to defend himself in court and is still fighting new battles with the HRC. Radio talk show host and author Mark Steyn (who often fills in for Rush Limbaugh) was also prosecuted or rather persecuted by Canada's Human Rights Commission for denigrating Islam.[15]

UN RESOLUTION 16/18 - DEFAMATION OF RELIGIONS

The Organization of Islamic Cooperation (OIC), composed of fifty-six member states plus the Palestinian Authority, are the largest voting block in the UN.[16] Over a decade ago they introduced a resolution that made it a criminal offense to defame Islam, and it passed the Human Rights Council of the UN. America kept voting against it, however in 2010 something very odd occurred: the US State Depart-

49

ment got involved in this resolution. Hillary Clinton flew to Istanbul Turkey to co-chair a meeting in with OIC secretary-general Ekmeleddin Ihsanoglu to "tweak" the language of UN Resolution 16/18.[17] The following year Hillary invited leaders of the OIC to Washington DC to continue their work which became known as the Istanbul Process.[18] The next year they had a third meeting in London at Wilton Park.[19] After three years, a compromise was made which allowed America's Ambassador to the UN to vote in favor for the Resolution in 2013.

I invited Deborah Weiss, who is an expert on Resolution 16/18, onto my radio program a few times to discuss this topic. She is an attorney, a journalist, and a survivor of the 9/11 attack in New York. Deborah outlined the trouble this is going to cause for the world, including America. She explained that a UN resolution is not a law, however, the resolutions create pressure on nations to conform to the global standard. If a resolution keeps getting voted on and approved year after year, like Resolution 16/18, it places pressure on non-complying nations to conform to the international code. Those who do not line up are at risk of losing funding and aid from the UN.

Deborah also explained that in American law, you can only libel or slander a person who is alive. You cannot defame an ideology or a religion per se. Ideologies and religions are inanimate objects. They can't feel, speak, or talk. You can no more insult a religion than you can insult a wooden chair. The UN resolution will have a hard time standing up in a US court room, but just like the Johnson Amendment, the public might think they are restricted by law when that is not the case.

Europe is adopting defamation of religions into their laws. For example, Pastor James McConnell of Belfast in Northern Ireland has been criminally charged by the UK government for violating the Communications Act. In one of his sermons, McConnell made some statements about Islam which ruffled a few feathers. Government officials asked him to retract his statements. He has refused, and he is now having his day in court. His defense is that he did not incite hatred or encourage violence against Muslims. He expressed views about another religion, not in a personalized manner but in a generalized way.[20] I am not a lawyer and do not know how British law sees the difference between defaming a person or an ideology. We should be closely watching the outcome of Pastor McConnell's case as it will have sweeping consequences on pastors throughout Europe.

ISLAM IS THE ENEMY, THE MUSLIM IS NOT

I say it often, "Don't blame Muslims for Islam." Muslims do what they do because of Islam. I hope it is becoming clear to you that Muslims are also victims of Islam. Islam not only victimizes those outside of Islam, the *Kufr*, but it also victimizes those inside. They never know if they have done enough to please Allah to earn their salvation. Allah

51

is the capricious one, the unknowable one. Not only can he change his mind but he can also change his nature. They cannot relate to Allah for he is un-relatable. The only guarantee a Muslim has to get to paradise is to die performing Jihad.

I must stress this point, Muslims do what they do because of Islam. The militant Muslim is a product of Islam not the root cause of Islam. If you remove Islam out of the Muslim you will have a benign, peaceful person.

I can illustrate it this way. Liberals want us to believe that guns are evil and they kill. If that is the case, I don't know how anyone survives a county gun show. The truth is, guns don't kill; angry people kill using guns or anything they can use as a weapon. Guns don't load, aim, and shoot by themselves. The gun is just the instrument; the evil is within the shooter. England has banned guns, but they still have problems with murders so now they are campaigning to take away knives. The liberal refuses to see that the evil is in the man. Just like the gun is the instrument, the Muslim is the instrument who is guided to do evil through the ideology of Islam.

PART TWO: DIVIDE THE RELIGION FROM THE SHARIAH

It has already been said that Muhammad was building more than just a religion; he was building a Kingdom. It is essential that we understand the significance of this fact. It means that Islam is more than just a religion.

To some extent we could say the same of the Jews. Jehovah God gave the Levitical laws to the priest in how temple worship was to be conducted. But he also gave the Jews laws to manage family life and civil life. There were dietary laws, criminal laws, trade and commerce laws. There were laws to operate a government, courts, finances, and even a military.

Since God did this for the seed of Isaac, Muhammad patterned the same with his god, Allah, for the seed of Ishmael, the Arabs. The *Shariah* goes further as it covers just about every part of the Muslim's life. For goodness sake, it even gives laws on how you are to go to the bathroom.

Dr. Bernard Lewis is without question the greatest academic authority on the Middle East. He is Professor Emeritus of Princeton University and author of twenty-five scholarly works on Islam and the Middle East. From studying his work, it would be safe to say that Muhammad saw that he lived in a kingdom without a king, unlike his Arab neighbors in Egypt and Syria. These neighboring kingdoms were more advanced in commerce, trade, military, and education because they had a centralized government. Arabia was broken into factions of three hundred and sixty tribes. Muhammad seized the opportunity to bring leadership to a superstitious people. By claiming to be a prophet of God he was able to bring Arabia together under Islam.

The Shariah is largely made up of laws to govern a nation. This is the portion of the Shariah that is up for debate and is not protected under religious freedom. By challenging the merits of the Shariah we are not debating or opposing a religion but rather an ideology. Therefore no holds are barred to us if we operate from this position.

I hope you can see how powerful this is in refuting Islam. In fact, using this tactic gives us a platform that can cripple Islam in America. If Islam is allowed to hide under the cloak of a religion they have protection under the First Amendment. We can rip away this protection and drive home the point that Islam is more than just a religion. Muhammad was not only giving birth to a religion, he was also establishing a kingdom that has a military component, a finance component, an education component, a legal component, and a governing component.

THE COLOR OF RELIGION

Another argument that can be made is that the First Amendment does not apply to Islam. The historic record is very clear that when our founders spoke of religion, they were referring to the Christian religion. The writers of the First Amendment knew that there were false religions in other nations but they were so foreign to our custom that they didn't even consider that clarification would be necessary. With that said, some (such as Patrick Henry) felt that clarification would be helpful.

As drafts of the Bill of Rights were being scribed, the framers sent letters back and forth discussing the wording. Patrick Henry proposed an exception clause to be in the First Amendment so that those who would use the 'Color of

Religion' to harm persons or property would not be granted freedom in this nation. It was similar to what was proposed in the Virginia constitution below.

Proposed draft for Virginia Article 15 and 16:

*'That no free government, or the blessings of liberty, can be preserved to any people but by a firm adherence to Justice, moderation, temperance, frugality, and virtue, and by frequent recurrence to fundamental principles. That religion, or the duty we owe to our Creator and the manner of discharging it, can be directed only by reason and conviction, and not by force or violence; and, therefore, that **all men should enjoy the fullest toleration in the exercise of religion**, according to the dictates of conscience, unpunished and unrestrained by the magistrates, **unless, under the color of religion, any man disturb the peace, the happiness, or the safety of society;** and that it is the mutual duty of all to practice Christian forbearance, love, and charity toward each other."*

It did not make it into the approved Virginia State Constitution but it was adopted into the Maryland Constitution.

Approved Maryland Article 37:

*"That as it is the duty of every man to worship God in such manner as he thinks most acceptable to Him, **all persons are equally entitled to protection in their***

> *religious **liberty**; wherefore, no person ought by any law to be molested in his person or estate, on account of his religious persuasion, or profession, or for his religious practice, **unless, under the color of religion, he shall disturb the good order, peace or safety of the State, or shall infringe the laws of morality, or injure others in their natural, civil or religious rights**; nor ought any person to be compelled to frequent, or maintain, or contribute, unless on contract, to maintain, any place of worship, or any ministry; nor shall any person, otherwise competent, be deemed incompetent as a witness, or juror, on account of his religious belief; **provided, he believes in the existence of God**...."*

This phrase, 'Color of Religion' is still in the Constitution of Maryland under Article 36.[21]

Whether it was the wisdom of the founding fathers or the providence of God, this exception was not in the final Bill of Rights. From my understanding it was argued that we have laws to protect persons and property and the exception clause was redundant.

Some would suggest that we try to get this phrase added to the First Amendment. Knowing the nature of politics I believe this would not be our best course forward without some work done to it. The vagueness of the exception clause is far too broad. Politicians and lawyers are too crafty at manipulating words to make them say something totally different from their original intent and we know they would use this clause against Christianity if at all possible. But we certainly have

56

ground to stand on in order to argue that the intent of the First Amendment was to protect the free practice of the Christian faith in America and perhaps the Christian faith exclusively.

The above argument is not a strong one to make and risky because it suggests that we amend our Constitution and I think we need to think long and hard before we start amending the Constitution. Therefore I suggest we navigate around the religious elements of Islam and attack the governmental part of the Shariah.

Dividing the *Shariah* from the religion navigates around the problem of freedom of religion for Islam. Don't attack the religion of Islam per se, rather address the *Shariah*. Acknowledge that our law allows Muslims to have their faith in Allah. Form your argument saying, "We are not forbidding Muslims to read the Qur'an or preventing them from building their Mosques, preforming the ablutions, saying their prayers, celebrating their feasts, fasting nor from going on their holy pilgrimages. The first amendment protects these practices because they are all part of their religion. However, we do have an issue with the *Shariah* of Islam."

The first 370 pages of the *Shariah* primarily deal with the laws of their religion and worship. The next 424 pages of the *Shariah* are the ones that don't have to do with the religion but with the government of Islam. The government of Islam, or the *Shariah,* is open for debate since they are not protected by the first amendment. It is with these aspects that we as patriots have the greatest issues.

CHAPTER SEVEN

BORROW CREDIBILITY

So you're not yet an expert on Islam. Don't worry about that, trust me, after reading this book you will have a better understanding of Islam than most Muslims in the world. I am always amazed at how little Muslims know about their own faith. Keep in mind, Islam is designed to keep the adherent ignorant. Knowledgeable people ask too many hard questions. The Qur'an is read in a language that over 80% of the Muslims can't read or write. Muslims memorize and parrot sounds in Arabic that they recite in prayers without even knowing what the words mean. In many Muslim nations, women are not permitted to learn how to read and write. An educated woman is a threat to an oppressive father or husband. If she is ignorant, she is dependent on them and therefore less independent.

In this chapter you will learn that you don't have to be an expert in order to speak with authority about Islam. I will teach you how to quote those who are experts, thus borrowing from their credibility. Let me give you an example of how this works:

Imagine you are a person who is well versed in America's darling sport, baseball. You are at the water cooler at work and a colleague spouts off a bunch of nonsense about a team. Your colleague is younger, less experienced, and you are seasoned, sensible, and well versed. You are a devoted fan of baseball, your card collection would be envied by Rick Harrison of Pawn Stars on the History Channel. But then this pimple faced colleague quotes sources you know and respect, Jon Miller and Bob Uecker, backing up his information. Now your judgment of this young colleague has changed. Instead of dismissing his information as twaddle, you now have an open mind on the subject. When you get home, you *google* the sources of his argument and to your chagrin you find out he was right.

This is borrowing credibility. When you cite the source of your information, you are no longer speaking from your own authority, but rather, you are borrowing their authority and credibility on the subject matter.

Everyone has an opinion about the issues of Islam. It is a popular topic around the water coolers and the break rooms of America. Much of it is filled with passion and sometimes anger. Some of what is discussed is inaccurate. Using the resources of this book, you can enter the debate with accurate, credible arguments.

Now let me caution you though, don't put yourself out there as the expert. We all have met him, the "know it all." He monopolizes the debate around the water cooler, and we are all nauseated by him. Don't be the know-it-all. Be discerning about how you share your knowledge, and do it in love and with patience.

The best English source I would recommend for refuting Islam is not the Qur'an nor is it the Sunnah. It is the classic Manual of Islamic Sacred Law. Entitled the 'Reliance of the Traveller' (ROT). When I quote from the Qur'an or from the Sunnah, I usually get accused of lifting verses out of context. It is tedious work to prove that I am not quoting a verse out of context. Sometimes after I prove I am using the verse in context, the point of citing the verse gets lost. Using the ROT eliminates this accusation and adds credibility to my argument.

The ROT will state a law, interpret what the law means, and often give the source for the law which will always be the Qur'an and/or the Sunnah. In addition, it will sometimes quote a famous scholar for authority. When I quote the ROT, I get the verses of the Qur'an, the Sunnah, plus Islam's highest scholars interpreting the verse for me. This is power, and I am borrowing from their credibility.

Using the ROT has another great function. It is a wonderful tool which allows us to use their own words against them. I have said for years, if Americans really knew what was in the *Shariah*, they would passionately resist it. The *Shariah* uncovers the ugly agenda of Muhammad. It exposes Islam as an oppressive, enslaving dictatorship. Muslims hate it when I use the ROT because it exposes the ugly, dark side of Islam and they have no rebuttal.

I will be giving you my *Cliff Notes* version on the ROT. You may want to purchase the ROT if you wish to be seriously engaged in the debate. They can be found for sale on Amazon for around $30 (ISBN 978-0-915957-72-9). With that said, you will find all the necessary material you will want to use from the ROT in this book, so it is not necessary to purchase a copy of the ROT. There are PDF versions of the ROT available online; just google "Reliance of the Traveller PDF."

In the next chapter I will teach you how to use the ROT and how to form arguments for refuting Islam with the evidence it contains.

CHAPTER EIGHT

USE THEIR WORDS AGAINST THEM

INTRODUCTION TO THE ROT

Shortly after Muhammad's death deep schisms began to form among the followers of Islam. The first rift was over succession. The *Shi'ites* believed that the Caliph (successor to Muhammad) should be of the blood line of the Prophet like in any royal family. The *Sunni's* believed it had to be the will of Allah to choose the successor and that being in the blood line was not necessary. Further divisions developed over the interpretation of the law and various schools of thought were formed. This is called jurisprudence or *madhhab*.

Schools of Islamic

Jurisprudence

Sunni	Shi'a
Shafi'i	Ja'fari
Hanafi	Zaydi
Maliki	

Hanbali	

Eight out of ten Muslims are going to be *Sunni* in doctrine, and the earliest and largest school of Islamic jurisprudence was *Shafi'i*. Because the *Shafi'i* school dates back to the founding Caliphs, they are considered the most accurate, or fundamentalist school. However, the most popular and now the largest Madhhab is *Hanafi*. The *Hanafi* Madhhab was largely influenced by the Ottoman Empire, and I would describe them as the reformers of Islam. The remaining schools are significant but not influential.

With this said, at the turn of the 15th century, there was a conference of the various Madhhabs. They debated the *Shariah* and came to a consensus that they agreed with each other about three quarters of the time. The one Madhhab that seemed to win the day was the *Shafi'i* school, and Anmad ibn Naqib al-Misri compiled a Manual of Islamic law as a result of the conference. In 1991 an American Muslim scholar translated the ROT into English and added his commentary and appendices to the work.

The ROT is well indexed and split into sections. Each chapter is alphabetized from A to Z. The first few chapters are introductory:

CHAPTERS A THROUGH D

Pages 1-100 discuss the sources of sacred knowledge, the importance of following qualified scholarship, an introduction, and methods used by the author to create the Manual of Islamic Law.

CHAPTERS E THROUGH J

Pages 101-370 discuss the sacred law and theology of the religion. They cover the purification and ablutions for worship. The Salat (Prayers), individual prayers, group prayers, Friday prayers, etc. are ordered. They give the rulings about the Zakat which is the alms giving. Chapter I deals with the laws of fasting and Chapter J is dedicated to the *Hajj* which is the pilgrimage to Mecca. These are basically the laws for worship which are commonly called the five pillars of Islam.

CHAPTER K THROUGH S

Pages 317-795 cover many different subjects, therefore, it will be easier to simply list them. I want you to understand that these are the issues outside of worship to a deity. They are laws to manage society, civil, family, education, courts, business, crime, and government. This is what I call government laws.

Chapter K	*Trade*
Chapter L	*Inheritance*
Chapter M	*Marriage*
Chapter N	*Divorce*
Chapter O	*Justice*

Chapter P	*Enormities (Sins)*
Chapter Q	*Command the Right and*
	Forbidding the Wrong
Chapter R	*Holding Ones Tongue*
Chapter S	*Delusions*

CHAPTER T THROUGH V

Pages 796-825 address some additional religious laws. The chapters are A Pure Heart, The Gabriel Hadith (traditions), and The Necessity for Belief in Allah and Muhammad.

CHAPTERS W THROUGH Z

Pages 826-1223 is where we find the last four chapters. They cover: Notes, Appendices, Biographical notes, Index and Citations.

HOW TO USE THE ROT

First we want to show the credibility this book has in the Islamic world.

- It is the oldest complete work of the *Shariah*.

- It is held in high regard by many Muslim Scholars. Endorsement Stamps from:

    o Sheikh Abd alWakil Durbui (Imam of Damascus, Syria) Page xiv o Sheikh Nuh Ali Salman (Mufti of the Jordanian Armed Forces) Page xvi

o Dr. Taha Jabir al-Alwani, President of International Institute of Islamic Thought and the Fiqh Council of North America. Page xvii-xix

o Certified by the noble Al-Azhar University Page xx-xxi

The last mentioned certification is perhaps the highest honor and most prestigious approval in the group. It is the stamp from the Al-Azhar University in Cairo, Egypt. If Islam had an Ivey league of schools, this institute would set the standard by which all others are measured. Founded in the year 970, it is the oldest degree granting Islamic University. In 2009, President Obama went to Egypt, the largest Arabic country in the world, to address the Islamic world. His platform was the esteemed Al-Azhar University.[22] If you are a graduate of Al-Azhar, you are considered the 'crème de la crème' of Imams.

Now we need to learn how to cite the references in the ROT. The ROT is cataloged with a *letter.number* sequence.

For example:

c3.0 OBLIGATORY ACTS

c3.1 ('Abd al-Wahhab khallaf:) Obligatory acts are distinguished in four ways, according to various considerations. One distinction is whether ....

c3.2 A second distinction between obligatory acts is made on the basis of who is called upon to perform them, namely whether an act is personally obligatory or communally obligatory. A personally obligatory (fard al-'ayn) act is ....

c3.3 A third way Obligatory acts are distinguished is by the amount of them required, that is, whether the act is of a defined amount or an undefined amount. Obligatory acts of defined amount are....

If you were to cite Islam's teaching on *Qibla*, the direction in which Muslims face when praying, you would reference it f6.0 Section F is all about the *Salat* (prayers). The number six is the sixth topic in this chapter. The zero is referencing the title of that section. There are seven subsections in f.6. If you were to discuss the *Shariah* on what to do if one learns they have prayed in the wrong direction, you would cite f6.7.

In writing you would proceed it with ROT. For example: ROT f6.7

Some portions are not translated into English. For example f6.4 is available to be read in the Arabic but for some reason the translator, Nuh Ha Mim Keller, chose not to translate it.

On occasion you get commentary added to the translation. This is referenced with an upper case letter followed by a colon all in brackets. There are only three commentators in the ROT:

> *A: References commentary by Sheikh Abd al-Wakil Durubi*
>
> *N: References commentary by Sheikh Nuh 'Ali Salman*
>
> *O: References commentary by Sheikh 'Umar Barakat*

Example:

> *ROT m7.5 When a (A: non-Muslim) man who has more than four wives becomes Muslim, he is obliged to choose just four of them (A: and the others' marriages are annulled).*

Sheikh Durubi adds some commentary at the beginning and the end of the ruling. He adds clarity that this ruling is pertaining to a non-Muslim. The comment at the end is explaining that the marriages to wives five, six, seven..... are simply annulled, there is no need to divorce the extra wives.

There are a couple more abbreviations that I should explain.

- (dif:)   meaning defined in another ruling

- (dis:)   meaning discussed in another ruling.

Example:

> *ROT m7.1 In any of the following circumstances, the husband or wife has the option to annul the marriage agreement immediately, if this is done in the presence of the Islamic magistrate (O: or a third party chosen to judge between them (dis: o21.4), provided that he is a mujtahid (def: o22.1(d)) and there is no Islamic judge), even when the partner annulling the marriage has the same defect whose existence in the spouse has motivated him or her to annul it*

Umar Barakat is adding some commentary to help the understanding. A ruling on a third party is discussed in the section of Justice at o21.4 and mujtahid is defined in o22.1 part (d)

One final thing I want to point out before we get into the real scandalous material of the *Shariah*. Pay attention to the quotation of the Qur'an and Sunnah from the ROT. The verses used here are in context and also interpreted for us. So if you use the verses straight out of the Qur'an, you can back up your point by referencing them being cited in the ROT.

Example:

I will often quote Surah 9:29 from the Qur'an,

> *Fight those who believe not in Allah nor the Last Day, nor hold that forbidden which hath been forbidden by Allah and His Messenger,*

nor acknowledge the religion of Truth, (even if they are) of the People of the Book, until they pay the Jizya with willing submission, and feel themselves subdued.

This verse clearly instructs Muslims to perform Jihad against those who do not believe in Islam. I can confirm I am correct in my interpretation because the ROT cites this verse when defining the objectives of Jihad in o9.8

Now with those explanations behind us we can get to the important stuff. Perhaps this next section is the reason why you purchased this book.

PART III : MAKING OUR CASE

CHAPTER NINE

ISLAM, AN IDEOLOGY OF VIOLENT CONQUESTS

The following chapters will outline arguments we can make in building our case against Islam. The evidence laid out in this chapter will be damaging to the reputation of Islam. Islam is more an ideology than it is a religion. It was invented by a man, and it is masquerading as a religion. In this chapter we are going to cover the subject of Jihad. We begin with the legal definition of Jihad.

ROT o9.0 JIHAD

> **"Jihad means to war against non-Muslims, and is etymologically derived from the word mujahada signifying warfare to establish the religion.** *And it is the lesser jihad. As for the greater jihad, it is spiritual warfare against the lower self, which is why the Prophet (Allah bless him and give him peace) said as he was returning from jihad."*

> ``We have returned from the lesser jihad to the greater jihad."

> *The scriptural basis for jihad, prior to scholarly consensus (def: b7) is such Koranic verses as:*

75

(1) `` *Fighting is prescribed for you"* *(Koran 2:216);*

(2) `` *Slay them wherever you find them"* *(Koran 4:89);*

(3) `` *Fight the idolators utterly"* *(Koran 9:36);*

and such hadiths as the one related by Bukhari and Muslim that the Prophet (Allah bless him and give him peace) said:

`` *I have been commanded to fight people until they testify that there is no god but Allah and that Muhammad is the Messenger of Allah,* *and perform the prayer, and pay zakat. If they say it, they have saved their blood and possessions from me, except for the rights of Islam over them. And their final reckoning is with Allah"*

and the hadith reported by Muslim,

`` *To go forth in the morning or evening* **to fight in the path of Allah is better than the whole world and everything in it."**

Details concerning jihad are found in the accounts of the military expeditions of the Prophet (Allah bless him and give him peace), including his own martial forays and those on which he dispatched others. The former consist of the ones he personally attended, some twenty-seven (others say twenty-nine) of them.

He fought in eight of them, and killed only one person with his noble hand, Ubayy ibn Khalaf, at the battle of Uhud. On the latter expeditions he sent others to fight, himself remaining at Medina, and these were forty-seven in number.)"

Here are the significant points of this section. Jihad is legally defined as *holy war*. The root of the word jihad comes from *Mujahada* just like the terrorist group the Mujahedeen out of Afghanistan.

Let me quickly explain the *greater* jihad and the *lesser* jihad. The *greater* jihad is the struggle of evil in one's life. Everyone has temptations, evil thoughts, and evil deeds. To fight or struggle against temptations is considered the *greater* jihad because everyone on the globe struggles in this battle. The *lesser* jihad is the war on the Kufr, the non-Muslim. It is limited to a region for a short time, so it is less in its scope. The *lesser* Jihad is no less important than the *greater* jihad, but as it is not worldwide, it is the *lesser* jihad.

Notice that this legal definition is consistent with the Qur'an and with the prophet of Muhammad. Also notice that this law is applicable for all faithful Muslims for all time; it has not been abrogated.

A quick comment about the two hadith sources quoted here from Bukhari and Muslim. The two most authoritative collectors of the sayings and traditions (hadith) of Muhammad were Bukhari and Muslim. They are often titled as Sahih meaning they are authentic and approved. It is like the *Textus Receptus* of the Greek New Testament, the commonly received text.

Let's continue with more shocking decrees about Jihad in the ROT.

> WHO IS OBLIGED TO FIGHT IN JIHAD
> *ROT o9.4 Those called upon to perform jihad when it is a communal obligation are **every able bodied man** who has reached puberty and is sane.*

> *THE OBJECTIVES OF JIHAD*

> *ROT o9.8 The caliph (o25) **makes war upon Jews, Christians, and Zoroastrians** (N: provided he has first invited them to enter Islam in faith and practice, and if they will not, then invited them to **enter the social order of Islam by paying the non-Muslim poll tax** (jizya, def: o11.4)-which is the significance of their paying it, not the money itself-while remaining in their ancestral religions) (O: and the war continues) until they become Muslim or else pay the non-Muslim poll tax.*

Note who they make war with: Jews and Christians. The Zoroastrians are a pagan group found in the Old Testament, and many still live today in Persia (Iran).

These following paragraphs from the ROT explain the law regarding the practice of Jihad, they speak for themselves and do not need my commentary.

THE RULES OF WARFARE

ROT o9.10 It is not permissible (A: in jihad) to kill women or children unless they are fighting against the Muslims. Nor is it permissible to kill animals, unless they are being ridden into battle against the Muslims, or if killing them will help defeat the enemy. It is permissible to kill old men and monks.

ROT o9.11 It is unlawful to kill a non-Muslim to whom a Muslim has given his guarantee of protection provided the protecting Muslim has reached puberty, is sane, and does so voluntarily

ROT o9.12 Whoever enters Islam before being captured may not be killed or his property confiscated, or his young children taken captive.

ROT o9.13 When a child or a woman is taken captive, they become slaves by the fact of capture, and the woman's previous marriage is immediately annulled.

Jihad is not just a doctrine in some law book. It is widely practiced among faithful Muslims which we would describe as terrorists. Some Muslims refer to Jihad as the sixth pillar of Islam as it is a compulsory duty. Muhammad gave high regard to Jihad by saying that one hour of Jihad equals up to sixty years of Salat (prayers).

"Standing for an hour in the ranks of battle is better than standing in prayer for sixty years." - *Saheeh related by Ibn Ade and Ibn Asakir from Abu Hurayrah 4/6165.*

Hadith: Sahih al Jaami as Sagheer no. 4305

Islam cannot escape the fact that it is a tyrannical, militant ideology that slaughters all who will not submit to it.

I have five more topics to cover in the Shariah. Each of these chapters are like truth torpedoes, capable of sinking Islam to the bottom of the sea. Christian patriots should load up on the vast ammunition the ROT provides for us to use against Islam.

CHAPTER TEN

ISLAM SUBJUGATES NON-BELIEVERS.

In this chapter we build a case from the ROT to show that Islam either demands the death of non-Muslims or subjugates them into a class system of Dhimmitude. Dhimmitude is not slavery, but it is a close cousin of slavery.

Here are the declarations in the Shariah on this topic.

THE NON-MUSLIM POLL TAX

ROT o11.4 The minimum non-Muslim poll tax is one dinar (n: 4.235 grams of gold) per person (A: per year). The maximum is whatever both sides agree upon. It is collected with leniency and politeness, as are all debts, and is not levied on women, children, or the insane.

ROT o11.5 Such non-Muslim subjects are obliged to comply with Islamic rules that pertain to the safety and indemnity of life, reputation, and property. In addition, they:

(1) are penalized for committing adultery or theft, though not for drunkenness;

81

(2) are distinguished from Muslims in dress, wearing a wide cloth belt (zunnar);

(3) are not greeted with "as-Salamu 'alaykum";

(4) must keep to the side of the street;

(5) may not build higher than or as high as the Muslims' buildings, though if they acquire a tall house, it is not razed;

(6) are forbidden to openly display wine or pork, to ring church bells or display crosses, recite the Torah or Evangel aloud, or make public display of their funerals and feastdays;

(7) and are forbidden to build new churches.

I don't want you to miss the significance of this

ROT o11.6 They are forbidden to reside in the Hijaz, meaning the area and towns around Mecca, Medina, and Yamama, for more than three days when the caliph allows them to enter there for something they need.

ROT o11.7 A non-Muslim may not enter the Meccan Sacred Precinct (Haram) under any circumstances, or enter any other mosque without permission.

ROT o11.8 It is obligatory for the caliph (def: o25) to protect those of them who are in Muslim lands just as he would Muslims, and to seek the release of those of them who are captured.

ROT o11.9 If non-Muslim subjects of the Islamic state refuse to conform

to the rules of Islam, or to pay the non-Muslim poll tax, then their agreement with the state has been violated o11.10 The agreement is also violated if the state has stipulated that any of the following things break it, and one of the subjects does so anyway, though if the state has not stipulated that these break the agreement, then they do not; namely, if one of the subject people:

(1) commits adultery with a Muslim woman or marries her;

(2) conceals spies of hostile forces;

(3) leads a Muslim away from Islam;

(4) kills a Muslim;

(5) or mentions something impermissible about Allah, the Prophet (Allah bless him and give him peace), or Islam.

ROT o11.11 When a subject's agreement with the state has been violated, the caliph chooses between the four alternatives mentioned above in connection with prisoners of war (o9.14).

We covered o9.14 under Jihad. The four options are:

- Death

- Slavery

- Release

- Held for Ransom

Dhimmitude is being practiced by ISIS on the Syrian Christians today. The Media Office of ISIS in Damascus released photographs showing dozens of Christians from the city of Al-Qaryaten signing the Dhimmi Contract requiring them to pay the poll tax and abide by Islamic rules. In return, under article eleven, ISIS will provide protection for them and their property. In the release, the following rules must be kept by the Dhimmis.

1.   Christians may not build churches, monasteries, or hermitages in the city or in the surrounding areas.

2.   They may not show the cross or any of their books in the Muslims' streets or markets, and may not use amplifiers when worshiping or during prayer.

3.   They may not make Muslims hear the reciting of their books or the sounds of church bells, which must be rung (sic) only inside their churches.

4.   They may not carry out any act of aggression against ISIS, such as giving refuge to spies and wanted men. If they come to know of any plot against Muslims, they must report it.

5. They must not perform religious rituals in public.

6. They must respect Muslims, and not criticize their religion.

7. Wealthy Christians must pay an annual jizya of four gold dinars; middle-class Christians must pay two gold dinars, and the poor must pay one. Christians must disclose their income, and may split the jizya into two payments.

8. They may not own guns.

9. They may not engage in commercial activity involving pigs or alcohol with Muslims or in Muslim markets and may not drink alcohol in public.

10. They may maintain their own cemeteries.

11. They must abide by ISIS dress code and commerce guidelines.[23]

PACT OF UMAR

Today, Christians in Syria are being forced to a humiliating subjugation under the threat to death. Ironically, Christians who lived in Syria 1,400 years ago suffered the same persecution and oppression from Islam.

The fore-mentioned rules by ISIS are similar to contract between the Patriarch of Jerusalem, Sophronius, and Islam's second Caliph, Umar ibn al-Khattab. In 637 AD, Umar's Army had just sacked Jerusalem and Bishop Sophronius pleaded the following terms in exchange for their lives.

> `In the Name of Allah, Most Gracious, Most Merciful. This is a document to the servant of Allah `Umar, the Leader of the faithful, from the Christians of such and such city. When you (Muslims) came to us we requested safety for ourselves, children, property and followers of our religion.

> We made a condition on ourselves that we will **neither erect** in our areas a monastery, church, or a sanctuary for a monk, **nor restore** any place of worship that needs restoration, nor use any of them for the purpose of enmity against Muslims.

> We **will not prevent any Muslim from resting in our churches** whether they come by day or night, and we will open the doors [of our houses of worship] for the wayfarer and passer-by. Those **Muslims who come as guests, will enjoy boarding and food for three days.**

> We will not allow a spy against Muslims into our churches and homes or hide deceit [or betrayal] against Muslims.

*We **will not** teach our children the Qur'an, publicise **practices of Shirk**, invite anyone to Shirk [i.e. **proselytise for Christianity**] **or prevent any of our fellows from embracing Islam,** if they choose to do so.*

*We will respect Muslims, **move from the places we sit in if they choose to sit in them.***

*We **will not** imitate their clothing, caps, turbans, sandals, hairstyles, speech, nicknames and title names, or ride on saddles, hang swords on the shoulders, **collect weapons of any kind or carry these weapons.***

We will not encrypt our stamps in Arabic, or sell liquor.

*We will have the front of our hair cut, **wear our customary clothes wherever we are, wear belts around our waist, refrain from erecting crosses** on the outside of our churches and demonstrating them and our books in public in Muslim fairways and markets.*

*We **will not sound the bells** in our churches, except discretely, **or raise our voices while reciting our holy books** inside our churches in the presence of Muslims, nor raise our voices [with prayer] at our funerals, or light torches in funeral processions in the fairways of Muslims, or their markets.*

We will not bury our dead next to Muslim dead, or buy servants who were captured by Muslims.

We will be guides for Muslims and refrain from breaching their privacy in their homes.'

When I gave this document to `Umar, he added to it, 'We will not beat any Muslim.'

These are the conditions that we [the Christians] set against ourselves and followers of our religion in return for safety and protection. If we break any of these promises that we set for your benefit against ourselves, then our Dhimmah [promise of protection] is broken and you are allowed to do with us what you are allowed of people of defiance and rebellion."'[24]

Perhaps the most famous verse in the Bible is John 3:16. Conversely, the most famous verse in the Qur'an is Surah 9:29 which cradles the conception of the Jizya, the non-Muslim poll-tax.

Fight those who believe not in Allah nor the Last Day, nor hold that forbidden which hath been forbidden by Allah and His Messenger, nor acknowledge the religion of Truth, (even if they are) of the People of the Book, until they pay the Jizya with willing submission, and feel themselves subdued.

The most prolific commentator of the Qur'an is Ibn Kathir in his Tafsir (commentary) of this verse he writes,

Paying Jizyah is a Sign of Kufr and
Disgrace.

*Allah said, (until they pay the Jizyah), if they
do not choose to embrace Islam, (with willing
submission), in defeat and subservience, (and
feel themselves subdued.),* **disgraced,
humiliated and belittled.** *Therefore, Muslims
are not allowed to honor the people of
Dhimmah or elevate them above Muslims, for
they are miserable, disgraced and humiliated.
Muslim recorded from Abu Hurayrah that the
Prophet said, (Do not initiate the Salam to the
Jews and Christians, and if you meet any of
them in a road,* **force them to its narrowest
alley.***) This is why the Leader of the faithful
`Umar bin Al-Khattab, may Allah be pleased
with him, demanded his well-known conditions
be met by the Christians, these conditions that*
**ensured their continued humiliation,
degradation and disgrace.**

The evidence against Islam is growing and it is very clear
that Islam is dangerous and destructive to American values.
However, there is even more distressing evidence that
needs to be revealed. I feel like a prosecutor who is about
to show his jury some very disturbing images. Some of the
evidence in the next chapter covers sexual abuse. Some of
the material I could not bring myself to include in this
book. Due to the graphic nature of some parts of the
Shariah I have judged that it is not necessary to cover every
dirty detail and have elected to omit them.

CHAPTER ELEVEN

ISLAM OPPRESSES WOMEN

Now let's explore the teachings of Islam and the Shariah when it comes to women. We can see many examples of women under oppression in Islamic countries like Saudi Arabia, where they are not allowed to drive cars[25] or be out in public with a man who is not a relative.[26] Also, in Pakistan girls are not allowed to go to school or learn how to read and write.[27] Again, the ROT provides us with ample evidence to make this case against Islam.

WOMEN ARE SEX OBJECTS FOR THE HUSBANDS.

> *ROT m10.11 (3) It is obligatory for a wife to obey her husband as is customary in allowing him full lawful sexual enjoyment of her person. It is obligatory for the husband to enable her to remain chaste and free of want for sex*

Note: This is consistent with the Qur'an in Surah 2:223

> *"Your wives are as a tilth unto you; so approach your tilth when or how ye will..."*

The meaning of *tilth* is a plowed field. Muslim scholars interpret this verse teaching the wife is a field for the man to plant his seed whenever and however he desires.

> *ROT m11.9 The husband is only obliged to support his wife when she gives herself to him or offers to, meaning she allows him full enjoyment of her person and does not refuse him sex at any time of the night or day.*

> *ROT w45.0   A   WIFE'S   MARITAL OBLIGATIONS*

> *ROT W45.1 A woman is not obliged to serve her husband by baking, grinding flour, cooking, washing, or any other kind of service, because the marriage contract entails, for her part, only that she let him enjoy her sexually, and she is not obligated to do other than that. (A: Rather, it is considered sunna in our school for the wife to do the housework, and the husband (who is obliged to support her) to earn the living, since this is how the Prophet divided the work between Fatima and Ali.*

ISLAM COMMANDS HUSBANDS TO BEAT THEIR WIVES.

Beating a disobedient wife is also consistent with the Qur'an in Surah 4:34.

Note: The following ruling is under section P which is for Enormities (Sins). These are grave crimes not just against man, but crimes against Allah.

*ROT p42.0 A WIFE'S REBELLING AGAINST
HER HUSBAND (def: m10.12)*

*ROT p42.1 Allah Most High says: "**Men are
the guardians of women,** since Allah has been
more generous to one than the other, and
because of what they (men) spend from their
wealth. so **righteous women will be obedient**,
and in absence watchful, for Allah is watchful.
And if you fear their intractability, **warn them,
send them from bed, or hit them.** But if they
obey you, seek no way to blame them" (Koran
4:34).*

*ROT p42.2 The Prophet (Allah bless him and
give him peace) said:*

*(1) "Allah will not look at a woman who is
ungrateful to her husband, while unable to do
without him."*

*(2) "When a man calls his wife to his bed and
she will not come, and he spends the night
angry with her, the angels, curse her until
morning."*

*(3) "It is not lawful for a woman to fast when
her husband is present, save by his leave. **Nor
to permit anyone into his house except with
his permission."***

*(4) "**Whoever leaves her husband's house (A:
without his permission), the angels curse her
until she returns or repents."***   *(Khalil*

Nahlawi:) *It is a condition for the*
permissibility of her going out (dis: m 10.3-4)
that she take no measures to enhance her
beauty, and that her figure is concealed or
altered to a form unlikely to draw looks from
men or attract them., Allah Most High says,
"Remain in your homes and do not display
your beauty *as women did in the pre-Islamic*
period of ignorance" (Koran 33.33)

WOMEN ARE FORCED INTO MARRIAGES.

Forced marriages are a growing problem for Muslim girls in Europe. The London Newspaper, *The Independent*, published a story of how Muslim girls cunningly escaped forced marriages. Thousands of British Muslim girls are being taken against their will to Asian countries in order to fill contracts of marriage arranged by their parents. To prevent this, many girls hid a spoon in their underwear hoping to be picked up by airport security. Then the girls would be taken to a private room where they could appeal to the authorities for protection from their parents. According to the newspaper, over 1,500 cases per year are being handled by the Forced Marriage Unit in Britain. Almost half of the incidents involved girls being taken to Pakistan. Over sixty countries were involved, and according to the paper the youngest girl was a two year old and the oldest was a seventy-one years old.[28]

> *ROT m3.13 Guardians are of two types, those*
> *who may compel their female charges to marry*
> *someone, and those who may not.*

(1)   The only guardians who may compel their charge to marry are a virgin bride's father or father's father, compel meaning to marry her to a suitable match (def: m4) **without her consent.**

FEMALE GENITAL MUTILATION (FGM)

The practice of FGM has become so common in the UK that the government has a dedicated unit to combat this crime. The British Government published a pamphlet on FGM which cites the results of a study by the World Health Organization. They estimate that three million girls undergo some form of procedure like this in Africa alone. It is practiced in twenty-eight countries and the British Government estimates that over twenty-thousand girls under the age of fifteen are at risk.[29]

> *ROT e4.3* **Circumcision is obligatory for both men and women.** *For men it consists of removing the prepuce from the penis, and for women,* **removing the prepuce of the clitoris**

> *Sunnahs: Abu Dawud, Adab 167   Abu al-Malih ibn `Usama's father relates that the Prophet said: "Circumcision is a law for men and a preservation of honour for women."*

WOMEN ARE HALF THE VALUE OF A MAN.

95

There are only two of the fifty-seven states in the OIC that give women equal testimony rights in their courts, they are Tunisia and Oman.[30]

Muhammad taught...

> ... *The women asked, "O Allah's Apostle! What is deficient in our intelligence and religion?" He said, "Is not the evidence of two women equal to the witness of one man?" They replied in the affirmative. He said, "This is the deficiency in her intelligence.*
>
> *Sahih Bukhari 1:6:301*

Females receive half the inheritance that a male would receive.

> *ROT L6.7 .... dividing this share so that each male receives twice the amount of each female*

When giving testimony in court, two women equal the strength of one man's testimony.

> *ROT m3.3 The second integral is that the marriage have witnesses, it not being valid unless two witnesses are present who are: (a) male (O: since a marriage witnessed by a man and two women would not be valid (A: though it would be valid in the Hanafi school));*
>
> *ROT o24.7 The testimony of the following is legally acceptable when it concerns cases involving property, or transactions dealing with property, such as sales:*

(1) two men;

(2) two women and a man;

(3) or a male witness together with the oath of the plaintiff.

ROT o24.8 If testimony does not concern property, such as a marriage or prescribed legal penalties, then only two male witnesses may testify (A: though the Hanafi school holds that two women and a man may testify for marriage).

*ROT o24.10 If testimony concerns things which men do not typically see (O: but women do), such as childbirth, then **it is sufficient to have two male witnesses, a man and two women, or four women.***

EXAMPLES OF OPPRESSION ON WOMEN (ROT)

ROT m11.3 The wife in entitled to what she needs of oil for her hair, shampoo and a comb or the like to stop underarm odor if water and soap will not suffice, and the price of water for her purificatory bath (ghusl) when the reason for it is sexual intercourse or the end of postnatal bleeding, though not if the reason is the end of her monthly period or something else (dis:m11.1).

ROT m11.4 The husband is not obliged (N: but rather is recommended) to pay for his wife's cosmetics, doctor's fees, the purchase of medicine for her, and similar expenses (A: though he must pay for expenditures connected with childbirth).

ROT m11.9 **The husband is only obliged to support his wife when she gives herself to him or offers to, meaning she allows him full enjoyment of her person and does not refuse him sex at any time of the night or day.** *She is not entitled to support from her husband when:*

(1) she is rebellious even if for a moment;

(2) she travels without his permission, or with his permission but for one of her own needs;

(3) she assumes ihram for hajj of `umra (def: j3);

(4) or when she performs a voluntary fast without her husband's permission.

ROT m13.4 **A woman has no right to custody of her child from a previous marriage** *when she remarries.*

ROT m6.7(5) **nor is it lawful or valid for a Muslim woman to be married to anyone besides a Muslim.**

*ROT p59.0 WOMEN WEARING FALSE HAIR
AND THE LIKE*

*ROT P59.1 The Prophet (Allah bless him and
give him peace) said, "Allah curse women who
wear false hair or arrange it for others, who
tattoo or have themselves tattooed, who pluck
facial hair or eyebrows or have them plucked,
and women who separate their front teeth for
beauty, altering what Allah has created."*

*ROT f12.4 ...It is better for women to pray at
home than at the mosque (A; whether they are
young or old). It is offensive for an attractive or
young woman to come to the mosque to pray
though not offensive for women who are not
young or attractive when this is unlikely to
cause temptation.*

*ROT f18.14.... It is offensive for women who
attend the Friday prayer to wear perfume or
fine clothes.*

*ROT m2.3 It is unlawful for a man to look at a
woman who is not his wife or one of his
unmarriageable kin, though part excludes her
voice, which is not unlawful to listen to as long
as temptation is unlikely. Allah Most High says,
``Tell believers to lower their gaze" (Koran
24:30).*

A majority of scholars have been recorded as holding the
position that it is unlawful for women to leave the house

with their faces unveiled, whether or not there is likelihood of temptation.

EXAMPLES OF OPPRESSION ON WOMEN (SUNNAH)

WOMEN ARE DEFICIENT IN INTELLECT.

> ... *"O people! Give alms."* Then he went towards the women and said. *"O women! Give alms, for I have seen that **the majority of the dwellers of Hell-Fire were you (women).**"* The women asked, *"O Allah's Apostle! What is the reason for it?"* He replied, *"**O women! You curse frequently, and are ungrateful to your husbands. I have not seen anyone more deficient in intelligence and religion than you**...*
>
> *Sahih Bukhari 2:24:541*

MUHAMMAD: WOMEN ARE THE INHABITANTS OF HELL.

> *Narrated Ibn 'Abbas: The Prophet said: "I was shown the **Hell-fire and that the majority of its dwellers were women** who were ungrateful."* ...
>
> *Sahih Bukhari 1:2:28*

> *Narrated Abu Said Al-Khudri: Once Allah's Apostle went out to the Musalla (to offer the prayer) o 'Id-al- Adha or Al-Fitr prayer. Then*

he passed by the women and said, "O women!
Give alms, as I have seen that the majority of
the dwellers of Hellfire were you (women)..."

Sahih Bukhari 1:6:301

*Narrated 'Abdullah bin Abbas: The people say,
"O Allah's Apostle! We saw you taking
something from your place and then we saw
you retreating." The Prophet replied... I also
saw the Hell-fire and I had never seen such a
horrible sight. I saw that most of* ***the
inhabitants were women.*** *" The people asked,
"O Allah's Apostle! Why is it so?" The*
Prophet replied, "Because of their
ungratefulness. *"Sahih Bukhari 2:18:161*

*Narrated Abu Said Al-Khudri: On 'Id ul Fitr or
'Id ul Adha Allah's Apostle (p.b.u.h) went out to
the Musalla. After finishing the prayer, he
delivered the sermon and ordered the people to
give alms. He said, "O people! Give alms."
Then he went towards the women and said. "O*
women! Give alms, for I have seen that the
majority of the dwellers of Hell-Fire were you
(women). *"*

Sahih Bukhari 2:24:541

*Narrated Usama: The Prophet said, "I stood at
the gate of Paradise and saw that the majority
of the people who entered it were the poor,
while the wealthy were stopped at the gate (for
the accounts). But* ***the companions of the Fire***

101

were ordered to be taken to the Fire. Then I stood at the gate of the Fire and saw that the majority of those who entered it were women."

Sahih Bukhari 7:62:124

MUHAMMAD COMPARED WOMEN TO DIRTY ANIMALS.

*Narrated 'Aisha: It is not good that you people have **made us (women) equal to dogs and donkeys.***

Sahih Bukhari 1:90:498

*Narrated 'Aisha: The things which annul the prayers were mentioned before me. They said, **"Prayer is annulled by a dog, a donkey and if a woman pass in front of the praying people."** I said, **"You have made us dogs."***

Sahih Bukhari 1:9:490

Is this the kind of lifestyle we want to see in to America? Those who sit on the fence about Islam, failing to form an opinion for or against Islam, do so because they are not being informed of the facts. America's silence and lack of resistance to Islam creates opportunity for Islam to get a foothold in our culture.

I find that, once people are informed with the facts, they are angered with Islam and motivated to take a stand. Remember, Muslims will not bend to our ways unless there is pressure upon them to do so. So far, Muslims are the ones applying the pressure, and we accommodate them to keep the peace. This needs to be reversed.

Christian Patriots need to take the floor and inform our countrymen about the truth of Islam. We need to apply pressure in the public forum to push back against Islam's destructive ideologies. If we remain silent, Muslims and liberals will take the floor and push their agenda. We can reverse the trend and take back ground that we have allowed them to take if we choose to do so. By studying this book you are taking the appropriate steps to be informed and armed with facts. Teach these truths to your friends, give this book or purchase copies for your friends or Pastors so they too can join a wall of resistance.

CHAPTER TWLEVE

ISLAM ENCOURAGES PEDOPHILIA

It is common knowledge that Muhammad married his favorite wife Aisha when she was only six years of age. He did not consummate the marriage until after her first period when she was nine and Muhammad was fifty-three. Aisha describes her mother preparing and dressing her for the wedding night with the Prophet....

> *Narrated Aisha:*
> *The Prophet engaged me when I was a girl of six (years). We went to Medina and stayed at the home of Bani-al-Harith bin Khazraj. Then I got ill and my hair fell down. Later on my hair grew (again) and my mother, Um Ruman, came to me while I was playing in a swing with some of my girl friends. She called me, and I went to her, not knowing what she wanted to do to me. She caught me by the hand and made me stand at the door of the house. I was breathless then, and when my breathing became all right, she took some water and rubbed my face and head with it. Then she took me into the house. There in the house I saw some Ansari women who said, "Best wishes and Allah's Blessing and a good luck." Then she entrusted me to them and they prepared me (for the marriage).*

105

> *Unexpectedly Allah's Apostle came to me in the forenoon and my mother handed me over to him, and at that time I was a girl of nine years of age.*
>
> *Sahih Bukhari 5:58:234*

A ruling in the chapter for marriage in the ROT stipulates that there is to be no difference in the marriage payment if the bride is a child. Child brides are paid for at the same price as adult brides.

> *ROT m8.2 A guardian may not marry **his prepubescent daughter** to someone for less than the amount typically received as marriage payment by similar brides, nor marry **his prepubescent son** to a female who is given more than the amount typically received. If he does either of these, the amount stipulated is void and the amount typically received is paid instead (O: in both these cases, as a necessary condition for the **validity of the marriage contract**).*

On divorce, a prepubescent child.

> *ROT n2.3 Neither sunna nor unlawful innovation means the **divorce of a wife who is prepubescent, postmenopausal**, pregnant, or one with whom one has not yet had sexual intercourse.*

On wet-nursing, it considers children who are able to nurse.

*ROT n12.1(a) the **milk comes from a female at** **least nine years old**, whether it is occasioned by sexual intercourse or something else;*

Here are some examples showing that in Islamic States the practice of pedophilia is still going on. In Yemen, an eight-year-old child bride died of internal bleeding sustained during her wedding night after being forced to marry a man five times her age.[31]

World Net Daily published a report earlier this year outlining some fatwas from some top Islamic scholars in the Middle East.

*"Grand Mufti, Abdulaziz is president of the Supreme Council of Ulema (Islamic scholars) and chairman of the Standing Committee for Scientific Research and Issuing Fatwas, which means he speaks authoritatively in Islamic teachings. Grand Mufti Abdulzaiz's more recent **ruling on marrying young girls** comes following a similar ruling in 2011 by Dr. Salih bin Fawzan, a prominent cleric and member of the Saudi's highest religious council, who issued a fatwa, or religious edict, that **there is no minimum age to marry girls, "even if they are in the cradle."**"[32]*

Mali (which is ninety percent Muslim) was the focus in a report by UNICEF. The report revealed that about 70,000 young girls aged between 9-12 years old, die each year as a result of child birth complications. The report called early marriage a "death sentence."[33]

The Problem with Equality

American courts now have a new measuring standard. The standard is no longer one of what is right and wrong, instead, it is now what is *equal*. Based on this new standard, the courts approved same-sex marriage because if a man and a woman have the right to marry each other, a man and a man or a woman and a woman should also have the right to marry each other, we cannot discriminate against them. Equal rights to all is the logic, and I predict polygamy will be coming real soon and then pedophilia. They will form arguments that we cannot discriminate against consenting adults, we cannot deny them their rights.

The pedophiles will argue that we cannot discriminate against people's age. A Child has as much rights to pleasures as an adult etc.....

We can expect liberals, who live in rebellion against God will try to make polygamy and pedophilia legal in America. However, we need to be aware that these two perversions are also promoted in the Shariah. It is likely that we will not see Muslims campaigning for these things to be made legal because the liberals will do this work for them.

We must stand against these efforts, the salt and light should rise up and oppose this nonsense. When should we fight this? After they get a foothold in the legal system and after it gains support from a non-discerning public? Or should we fight it before it gets a chance to incubate? I say we should follow the wise words from old Barney Fife, *"Nip it in the bud! You got to nip it in the bud! ... NIP IT!*

CHAPTER THIRTEEN

ISLAM PRACTICES SLAVERY

Under the section of Jihad in the ROT we see that those who are captured can be taken as slaves.

*ROT o9.13 When a child or a woman is taken captive, **they become slaves by the fact of capture**, and the woman's previous marriage is immediately annulled.*

*ROT o9.14 When an **adult male is taken captive**, the caliph considers the interests and decides between the **prisoner's death, slavery, release without paying anything, or ransoming himself in exchange for money or for a Muslim captive held by the enemy**. If the prisoner becomes a Muslim then he may not be killed, and one of the other three alternatives is chosen.*

Chapter eight of the Qur'an gives the rules for war booty. The fighters had to pay a tax on all they gained from the booty to Muhammad; this is called the Khums, which means a fifth. The Khums tax went to support the prophet and his household. When the Khums were paid in slaves, Muhammad got to choose the most desirable of the women and strongest of the men for his fifth. Most Americans have never heard of the white slavery that took place in Africa. There are a few books out on this topic. I recommend getting Robert C. Davis' book, *Christian Slaves, Muslim Masters* which is very comprehensive and scholarly. The opening chapter deals with the numbers of white slaves in Africa from the 1500's through the 1850's. Muslim pirates would capture ships and enslave crews from Iceland, England, France, Portugal, Spain, Italy, Holland, and America. Ohio State Professor Davis estimates over one million white men and women were captured and made slaves by Muslims of North Africa. According to the record, the treatment of these white slaves was brutal and disgraceful. I suspect that some white American slave owners may have been cruel to their black slaves to repay the ruthless treatment of white slaves by black African slave owners.

We should also note that the slaves who were brought from Africa were first captured and enslaved by black, Muslim tribes. Muslim warriors would travel inland to the central parts of Africa and raid villages to capture male and female slaves. Then they brought them to the coast to sell them to the slave ships bound for Europe and America. The point is that it was because of Islam, many Africans were enslaved and sold. This does not justify the injustice of slavery practiced by the Europeans and the Americans, but it does shed some light on this dark part of our history.

THE MUSLIM PRACTICE OF AL SABI

111

Al sabi is the doctrine of enslaving women for the purpose of sex for the Muslim fighters. The UN released a report from their Sexual Violence division concerning Syria. The report included testimony of girls who were able to escape ISIS. The report told the story of a nine year old girl who was sexually abused by at least ten ISIS fighters and became pregnant. There was also a nineteen year old who told of the horrors she witnessed. When ISIS came to her village, the men were given the choice to convert to Islam or be shot. The girls and the young women were separated and sold as sex slaves. They were taken to a building in Mosel which she described as a sex slave warehouse where hundreds of women and girls were held. They would line up about fifty of them in lines of ten and were told, "don't move, don't cry, or we will beat you." Men would enter to pick and choose as they pleased. She and a few other girls managed to escape that night.[34]

ISIS publishes a glossy online magazine called Dabiq. In the 9th Edition they carried an article entitled "Slave-Girls or Prostitutes?" by Umm Sumayyah Al-Muhajirah. Starting on page forty-four, the article outlined the justification from Islamic scriptures for the practice of sex slaves. Here is a brief synopsis of her argument, which is evidence we can quote to show the wickedness of Islam. The first authority quoted is the Qur'an:

Surah 23:5-6

And they who guard their private parts, except from their wives or those their right hands possess, for indeed, they will not be blamed}

The phrase "those their right hands possess" means they are slaves. This verse says that it is righteous to protect your private parts from all except two groups of people: your wives and your slaves. This is because you can have sex with both your wives and your slaves.

The next authority quoted is from the Sunnah.

Sa'īd Ibn Jubayr reported that Ibn 'Abbās (radiyallāhu 'anhumā) said, 'Approaching any married woman is fornication, **except for a woman who has been enslaved'***"*

An unbelieving woman's marriage is invalidated **when she becomes a captive and is enslaved. It is, therefore, not fornication to have sex with her.**

Now she quotes from the Sirat:

The Sīrah is a witness to our Prophet's raiding of the kuffār. He would kill their men **and enslave their children and women.** *The raids of the beloved Prophet convey this to us. Ask the tribes of Banī al-Mustaliq, Banī Quraydhah, and Hawāzin about this. The tribes spoken of here are the Jewish tribes betrayed by Muhammad.* **He beheaded the men and took the women and girls as sex slaves.** *This is called the Battle of the Trench.*

113

> *Banī Quraydhah yielded to the judgment of Saʾd Ibn Muʾādh. So Saʾd said, "**I rule that their fighters be killed and their families be enslaved.**" So Allah's Messenger said, "You have indeed judged in their affair by the ruling of Allah" [Reported by al-Bukhārī and Muslim]*

Here is another incident from the Sirat:

> *The number of Jews killed in the battles of Khaybar reached 93 men. Their women and children were enslaved, and Safiyyah Bint Huyayy Ibn Akhtab – the Mother of the Believers – fell into captivity. Allah's Messenger set her free and married her [Reported by al-Bukhārī and Muslim]. And during the expedition of Hunayn, **Allah's Messenger enslaved from Hawāzin until the amount of slaves reached six thousand.**

This is the final selection from the Sirat:

> ***Therefore, we almost cannot find a companion who didn't practice saby.*** *ʿAlī Ibn Abī Tālib had nineteen slave-girls. Ibn ʿUyaynah reported that ʿAmr Ibn Dīnār said, "ʿAlī Ibn Abī Tālib wrote in his will, 'As to what follows: If something happens to me during this battle, then my slave-girls whom I copulate with are nineteen in number. Some of them bore me children, some of them are pregnant, and some of them are childless'"*

In short, all of Muhammad's companions practiced al-sabi.

114

Muslims still practice slavery today in Africa, but it has been renamed for political correctness. Titles like "human trafficking" or "forced labor" are the new terms journalists use to speak about slavery. *The World Alliance Against Forced Labor* estimates that there are over six hundred thousand victims of slave labor in the Sub-Saharan region of Africa. Kira Salak, a writer for the National Geographic, showed that slavery is still going strong in Mali (ninety percent Muslim) when she bought two slaves and then freed them in Timbuktu.[35] In May of 2015, the BBC World Service posted that four percent of the population of Mauritania (all Muslim) are enslaved placing it at the top of the Global Slavery Index.[36] You don't have to dig too deep to find that slavery is still practiced widely by Muslims.

Let's ask those skeptics who sit on the fence about Islam if they support slavery. If you support Islam, you support slavery. Let's ask them if they support taking freedom away from others. Ask them if they want slavery practiced or freedom taken away from them in their community.

We have two more issues to cover in the Shariah, how Muslims are in bondage because of Islam and the issue of Apostasy.

CHAPTER FOURTEEN

ISLAM IMPRISONS THEIR ADHERENTS

In this chapter we are going to cover Islam's doctrines on apostasy. Most Nations build walls in order to keep people, whom they deem might be a threat to their society, out. You know you've got a good thing going when everyone wants to live in your country. On the flip side, you know you've got a bad thing going if you have a nation who builds walls to keep their people in. This is a prison. That's exactly what the USSR did in Berlin after World War II; they built a wall, not to keep the West Germans out, but to keep the East Germans in Communism.

Islam has built walls around Muslims with their doctrines of apostasy. The following passages out of the ROT will clearly reveal that anyone who leaves the faith of Islam is to be killed.

ROT o8.0 APOSTASY FROM ISLAM (RIDDA)

Leaving Islam is the ugliest form of unbelief (kufr) and the worst....

ROT o8.1 When a person who has reached puberty and is sane voluntarily apostatizes from Islam, he deserves to be killed.

ROT o8.2 In such a case, it is obligatory for the caliph to ask him to repent and return to Islam. If he does, it is accepted from him, but if he refuses, he is immediately killed.

ROT o8.3 If he is a freeman, no one besides the caliph or his representative may kill him. If someone else kills him, the killer is disciplined

ROT o8.4 There is no indemnity for killing an apostate

Muslims live in fear of their religion. They don't stay with Islam because they know in their hearts that Islam is the truth; many stay with Islam because someone will kill them if they renounce their faith. This is why many Muslims come to America but don't practice their faith. Since they have not renounced Islam, so they are not an apostate. They keep Islam at arm's length and call it their culture.

The first Caliph, Abu Bakr ruled for two years. He did not increase Islam's land holdings because he was busy fighting the Ridda (apostasy) wars. Many Arabs became Muslims under duress from Muhammad. When Muhammad died, they thought they could return back to their many gods. Abu brought the sword upon forty thousand apostates throughout Arabia over his two year reign, which made the Arabs submit to their imprisonment to Islam.

117

When Umar took the throne, he could concentrate on the Jihad of the Christians and Jews in Jerusalem and Syria.

One of Islam's top clerics preached on Al-Jazeera TV back in February of 2013 about the importance of penalizing apostasy. Sheikh Qaradawi bemoaned that the Islamic world is not carrying out the penalty for apostasy, and he made the greatest admission I have ever heard a Muslim cleric say. I am sure he did not mean it to be an admission. He said, "If they had gotten rid of the apostasy punishment, Islam wouldn't exist today."[37] Think about what he said. The only reason Islam exists today is because Muslims are threatened with death if they leave the faith. This is perhaps one of the strongest arguments we can make against Islam.

<u>CHAPTER FIFTEEN</u>

ISLAM IS ANTI-AMERICAN

It should be evident by now that Islam's core doctrine and mission is to bring the world into submission to Allah. Again, Islam means submit, surrender. This tenant is diametrically opposed to a core value of America which is liberty. Islam cannot rule the world if there is a democratic republic. Freedom to speak your mind, freedom to choose who you worship or if you worship at all does not exist in the Islamic model. Therefore, freedom and those who wish to live under liberty must be destroyed.

The style of government that Muhammad created is similar to that of Nazism, a Fascist government that rules by dictatorship with a supreme commander. This is why the Muslims joined ranks with Hitler. There were two Muslim *SS* divisions in the Balkans. If you search the internet you will find the Grand Mufti of Jerusalem making a pact with Hitler. By the way, the Anti-Christ will rule the world by a dictatorship.

I wish to prove that Islam is anti-America and I will demonstrate this by comparing Shariah law to our Bill of Rights. In order to be brief we are only going to examine the Shariah to the First Amendment of our Constitution. If America has a King it is the Constitution. We are a nation of laws and our Constitution is the bedrock for our laws.

120

Without it we are left with anarchy, therefore, it is vital to our nation that we cherish and protect our Constitution from all enemies foreign or domestic. When our President takes the oath of his office he promises to "...preserve, protect, and defend the Constitution of the United States." When US Congressmen and Congresswomen take an oath, they pledge these words as will our soldiers "I, _____, do solemnly swear that I will support and defend the Constitution of the United States against all enemies, foreign and domestic..."

Here is the First Amendment:

> *Congress shall make no law respecting an (1)establishment of religion, or prohibiting the free exercise thereof; or (2)abridging the freedom of speech, or (3)of the press; or the (4)right of the people peaceably to assemble, and to (5)petition the government for a redress of grievances.*

I have added numbers to point out there are five provisions or protections in this law. We will take each provision and compare them to Islam. Before we get to that comparison, I want to make an observation about this amendment. This law sets a restriction on those who make our laws and it provides protections for the people. It begins, *"Congress shall make no law respecting....."* Our Founders carefully studied the governments of other nations and of history. They learned that government, by nature, can be dangerous as it grants power and control to some, who often become

121

tyrants over the people. Forming a government of the people, by the people potentially could be dangerous, so, they needed to install restrictions to limit government's power and empower the people. (I wish I could take a diversion here and address the importance of the Second Amendment but I will let that rabbit get away this time.)

The First Amendment is *not* a restriction on the people, but rather a restriction on the government. It tells the government, that they are not going to establish a State religion and dictate who we call God or how we are going to worship him. The government is not going to limit what we can say or prohibit the Press from what they are going to investigate and report on. These are checks and balances on our government to keep them from gaining too much power and control. We want to preserve liberty in our religious choices and in our speech. We want our Press to be free to blow the whistle on corruption in the government if it is found. We also want the government to be prohibited from stopping any peaceful assembly and if our government is out of line, we demand the right to redress our grievances freely without fear of penalties.

The First Amendment is essential to the way of life in America. Without this law, we lose freedom. Anything that threatens this law that protects our liberty should be treated severely as an enemy of the State. It should be vigorously rooted out of the country and given no safe haven within our shores. With that said, now let's compare the doctrines and practices of Islam to the five provisions in the

First Amendment. We will keep score...I will award a point for each time Islam is in agreement with the five protections in the First Amendment.

1. **Establishment of religion, or prohibiting the free exercise thereof.**

We have already covered the sections of Jihad in chapter nine and Apostasy in the previous chapter. The evidence in the ROT is irrefutable that Islam violates these protections. Islam is established as the sole religion and if anyone leaves it, they do so under the sentence of death. The concept of freedom of religion in Islam is that you are free to choose Islam as your religion. This is not freedom but rather subjugation. Islam threatens the freedom we have guaranteed to us so we can choose who we worship or even if we worship at all. Look at Iran for example, you are thrown in jail if you are caught propagating the doctrines of Christianity. The same can be said of many other Islamic States.

No points here. Score is 0 - 5

2. **Freedom of Speech and Freedom of the Press**

A prime example of an assault on freedom of speech under Islam is the Danish Cartoon incident. Jyllands-Posten's goal was to exhibit freedom of speech, and that Denmark was not under Islamic control. The Publisher asked his readership to submit some drawings of the Prophet Muhammad to demonstrate their rights to freedom of speech and not self-censor themselves in compliance to Shariah.

Canadian journalist, Ezra Levant, was the only western reporter who covered the Danish Cartoon incident correctly. I had Ezra on my program to tell the story of how he was persecuted by the Human Rights Commission in Canada for daring to publish these cartoons. Most of the world is still ignorant of what really happened. Twelve drawings were published in the Jyllands-Posten which angered local Muslim clerics. They led rallies against the paper but the cartoons were not really that offensive and it did not create the outrage the Imams hoped for, so the clerics added three more images themselves. They took these three images to the Middle East to stir up trouble, falsely claiming they were published by the Danish paper. We have all the pictures on our website at www.fortressoffaith.org. Just type Danish Cartoons in the search bar to see the story and the pictures.

Two of the images that the Muslim clerics produced were not cartoons. They were photocopies of pictures with insulting words about Muhammad. One image was a photograph of a man wearing a pig's nose and pig ears with an Arabic caption, 'Here is the real image of Muhammad'. The other image is of a dog mounting the backside of a Muslim man while he was kneeling in prayer. The third drawing is of Muhammad in a sex orgy with little girls which we do not show on our website.

It is important to know that *none* **of these images were published or presented to the Newspaper. They were produced by the Imams to outrage and incite the Muslim community to riot.** By the way, the image of the man with a pig's nose and ears was a photograph from a French Newspaper. The paper was covering a pig–squealing competition which had nothing to do with the Danish cartoons or Muhammad.

Before my point gets lost, the protest and outrage from the Muslim world demonstrates how Islam feels about the freedom of speech. The New York Times reported of deaths from around the world due to the riots.[38] Some of the cartoonists were attacked, as was the editor of the paper and many had to go into hiding. We all remember the incident in Garland, Texas when two soldiers of ISIS tried to shoot their way in at the 'Draw Muhammad' event. The event was to demonstrate America's rights to free speech and Islam's faithful showed us they will not tolerate a Non-Muslim blaspheming their prophet. Islam does not permit freedom of speech.

A potential two points could have been gained here but none awarded. The score is still 0 - 5

3. Freedom to Assemble and make Petitions against Grievances.

I refer you back to Chapter Ten and the Pact of Umar. Non-Muslims living under Islamic rule are Dhimmis, a lower caste system which is just a breath away from slavery. Non-Muslims have limited rights to freely assemble and it is laughable to think Non-Muslims would have the right to redress the Caliph with a list of grievances.

Another two points could have been awarded here but none can be allotted as Islam violates all five provisions given to protect freedom and liberty in the First Amendment. The score is zero to Islam and five to Liberty.

In short. Islam is anti-American. We have two United States Congressmen who are Muslims, Keith Ellison from Minnesota and Andre Carson from Indiana. How can Muslims swear an oath to protect the Constitution when it violates principles of Islamic doctrine? Either they are loyal to Islam or they are loyal to our Constitution. You cannot have it both ways.

By the way, neither of these men swore on the Holy Bible when they gave their oath into office. They were sworn in on the Qur'an that Thomas Jefferson purchased in London in order to understand why Muslims were attacking our ships. This is contemptuous to our way of life and values.

Christianity was the source behind American laws. We can find examples of how the protections in the First Amendment are Biblical precepts. The New Testament apostle's would meet in the market places which displays the right to peaceably assemble. The story of Ester is a great example of petitioning the government for redress. The freedom to choose not to worship and obey Jehovah is clear from the beginning in Genesis. God could have made mankind robots without a free will but instead he gave mankind the freedom to choose obedience or disobedience. Every parent knows the joy it brings when their children choose to follow their wishes. We are thankful when they obey, but it is far better when they willingly obey without being forced to comply. Thus we can understand why God gave us a free will to demonstrate our loyalty and devotion. Anything else would be servility.

For the most part we have been dealing with the political social issues of Islam. Now let's shift gears and deal with the religious, theological issues of Islam. I am a Christian preacher trained in Christian theologies for the ministry of missionary work. However, this last decade I have devoted myself to the study of the '*ologies*' of Islam, its faith and practice.

The upcoming subjects I am about to address will be of great interest to Christian apologists, evangelists and missionaries. Avi Lipkin, a Jewish politician in the Knesset said to me, over a bowl of spaghetti at the *Olive Garden*, "If we don't win them to the Lord, they [Muslims] will destroy us with the sword." We have to address the root of the problem with Muslims which is their faith in Islam. We must help them to understand that Muhammad was a false prophet and the truth of Christ is lost in the Qur'an. The only way to change them is to introduce them to the truth of the Holy Bible.

I hope that I don't lose some of my readers at this point. Perhaps you are not a person of faith, and you don't believe in Christ. You must understand that Islam creates people of faith, so to refute Islam, you have to understand the faith issue. Perhaps the next few chapters will help you understand not only the faith of Muslims but also the faith of Christians.

CHAPTER SIXTEEN

MUSLIMS TOP OBJECTIONS TO CHRISTIANITY

Three common objections that come up when giving the gospel to Muslims are: Preservation of the Holy Bible, the Deity of Christ, and the Crucifixion.

Samuel Zwemer is perhaps the most popular missionary to Muslims in American history. The institute that bears his name said that less than one percent of all missionaries throughout Christianity are targeting Muslims. This means that Christians are largely ignoring one-fourth of our world, this is disgraceful. The best place to evangelize Muslims is in North America where we don't have apostasy laws prohibiting us from reaching them. Many Muslims are here because they want to get away from Islam and Muslim apostates are not likely to be killed as they would be in Islamic countries. You may not have many Muslims in your community now, but just wait five to ten years; you are sure to have more, so let's learn how to give an answer to Muslim objections about our faith.

REFUTING THEIR CLAIM THAT THE HOLY BIBLE IS CORRUPT

129

For this section, I am going to cut and paste from a tract I wrote in order to answer this question. I entitled the tract "Are Muslims Forbidden to read the Holy Bible? The Modern Cleric will say, 'Yes,' but the Prophet Muhammad would say 'No!'" You will see that the Qur'an says the Holy Bible is inspired and guarded from corruption.

Modern clerics say things about the Holy Bible that Muhammad would not say. They say that Christians and Jews have corrupted the Bible and that it is no longer trustworthy. However, this is not what Muhammad would have said, and it is certainly not taught in the Qur'an. Muhammad would not teach anything contrary to the Qur'an, but Modern Clerics do.

The Qur'an says that there was a group of Christians who distorted the Bible with their "tongues" (Surah 3:78), but it does not say that the Bible text was distorted.

What does the Qur'an say about the Bible?

1. Christians are to stand by their Scriptures.

Surah 5:68 "O People of the Book! ye have no ground to stand upon unless ye stand fast by the

Law, the Gospel, and all the revelation that has come to you from your Lord."

Why would Muhammad tell Christians to stand on Scriptures that were corrupt?

2. There is no difference between the Bible and the Qur'an.

Surah 2:136 "We believe in Allah, and the revelation given to us, and to Abraham, Isma'il, Isaac, Jacob, and the Tribes, and that given to Moses and Jesus, and that given to all prophets from their Lord: We make no difference between one and another of them:"

Therefore, Muslims are to give reverence to the Holy Bible.

3. The Bible is inspired of God.

Surah 21:7 "Before thee, also, the messengers We sent were but men, to whom We granted inspiration: If ye realise this not, ask of those who possess the Message."

Inspiration prevented man from making a mistake when transmitting God's word to paper.

4. The Scriptures will be kept from corruption. This includes the Bible.

Surah 15:9 "We have, without doubt, sent down the Message; and We will assuredly guard it from corruption."

Surah 5:48 "To thee We sent the Scripture in truth, confirming the scripture that came before it, and guarding it in safety."

What Scriptures came before "it" (Qur'an)? The Bible! The Bible is confirmed and guarded in safety. So in short, the Qur'an says the Bible is inspired and preserved from corruption.

If Allah is powerful enough to keep man from corrupting the Qur'an, why was he not powerful enough to keep man from corrupting the Bible? This is a major flaw in Islamic doctrine. If the Bible and the Qur'an have the same author, we should have unity in doctrine, but we don't. Muslims in Muhammad's day did not have access to the Bible to check out Muhammad's claims. If they did, they would have rejected Muhammad as God's prophet.

Imams hope you will never discover the truth in this pamphlet. Muslims know it's forbidden to question the Qur'an and no mercy is given to anyone who questions it. Clerics don't want you to read the Bible for the same reason Satan doesn't want you to read the Bible: you might believe and be saved.

Luke 8:12 "then cometh the devil, and taketh away the word out of their hearts, lest they should believe and be saved."

Read the Bible, and ask the God of Abraham to speak to you through it. Start in the Gospel of

John which was written by a disciple of Jesus Christ.

The Bible, like the Qur'an, speaks of Biblical inspiration and preservation.

2 Peter 1:21 "For the prophecy came not in old time by the will of man: but holy men of God spake as they were moved by the Holy Ghost."

2 Timothy 3:16 "All scripture is given by inspiration of God."

1 Peter 1:25 "But the word of the Lord endureth for ever."

There has been a pure, consistently recurring text known as the Textus Receptus. The purity of God's Word can be traced and documented through thousands of manuscripts that date over two thousand years. The King James Version of the Bible is the oldest and the most accurate English translation of the Textus Receptus. One empirical proof is the 1946 discovery of the Dead Sea Scrolls found in the caves of Qumran by a Muslim shepherd boy. These 981 scrolls of Hebrew Scriptures were penned in 400 BC and hidden for fifteen hundred years, yet they match our Bible word-for-word.

So, what is the message that the God of Abraham wants mankind to know?

God wants to reveal Himself to us: His Power and Authority, His Holiness, His Righteous Law, His Justice, His Love, His Grace and His Mercy.

As you study God's Word, you quickly see that man willfully chose to disobey God. God calls this sin, and every sin is a serious offense against God. He awards death as the penalty for sin. This is seen throughout the Bible.

Genesis 2:17 "But of the tree of the knowledge of good and evil, thou shalt not eat of it: for in the day that thou eatest thereof thou shalt surely die."

Romans 5:12 "Wherefore, as by one man sin entered into the world, and death by sin; and so death passed upon all men, for that all have sinned:"

Adam and Eve did not die physically that day, but they died a spiritual death. It is our sin that separates us from God. We can be pardoned from our guilt of sin through the right blood sacrifice.

Leviticus 17:11 "For the life of the flesh is in the blood: and I have given it to you upon the altar to make an atonement for your souls: for it is the blood that maketh an atonement for the soul."

Romans 3:25 "Whom God hath set forth to be a propitiation through faith in his blood."

Propitiation means payment: a payment in full. A blood sacrifice is what God accepts to put us in right standing with Him again. Who is this person in verse 25? The preceding verse tells us that it is Jesus Christ.

Vs.24 "Being justified freely by his grace through the redemption that is in Christ

Jesus."

Only the sacrificial blood of a sinless man could atone and pay the debt of man's sin. That perfect sacrifice was God in the flesh. The Bible calls Jesus "Emmanuel" meaning God with us (Matt. 1:23).

Christians are not making a man into a God so this is not "shirk" or blasphemy. God took on flesh and became a man. This is not impossible for God, as all things are possible to Him within His holy nature. Friend, you can never merit God's pardon by your good deeds. Forgiveness cannot be earned.

Eph 2:8-9 "For by Grace are ye saved through faith; and that not of yourselves: it is the gift of God: Not of works, lest any man should boast."

The gift of God is the blood shed by Jesus Christ to pay for the debt of your sin.

John 3:16 "For God so loved the world, that he gave his only begotten Son, that whosoever believeth in him should not perish, but have everlasting life."

God is to be feared. If you reject God's gift, you will have to pay for your own sin debt in the lake of fire for all eternity (Revelation 20:15).

Repent of your self-righteousness; by faith, accept the blood of Jesus Christ to pay your sin debt. Renounce Islam and profess Jesus as your Savior.

REFUTING THEIR CLAIM THAT JESUS IS NOT GOD

This section could also be used for Mormons and Jehovah's Witnesses as they, like the Muslims, reject the deity of Jesus Christ. Muhammad said that the greatest sin is "Shirk", which is making someone or something a partner with God. Muhammad claimed that Christians commit shirk by making Jesus a God.

However, this is not what the Bible teaches; rather it teaches that God became a man. The angel Gabriel said his name is "Emmanuel, God with us" (Matt 1:23). The Bible teaches us that Christ "took on flesh and dwelt among us" (John 1:14). Christ's deity is perhaps the most important to our knowledge of God. God is a triune being: three persons yet still one.

Some erroneously assert that Jesus never claimed to be God. He did not utter the words, "I am God," but he certainly communicated it and those around Him understood clearly what He was saying. Five times Christ was accused of blasphemy because He was communicating that He was God. Blasphemy is a serious charge, a capital offense with the sentence of death by stoning (Lev 24:16). Let's take a look at what Jesus said that caused the Pharisees to accuse Him of blasphemy.

Mark 2:5-10

*When Jesus saw their faith, he said unto the sick of the palsy, Son, thy sins be forgiven thee. 6 But there were certain of the scribes sitting there, and reasoning in their hearts, 7 **Why doth this man thus speak blasphemies? who can forgive sins but God only?** 8 And immediately when Jesus perceived in his spirit that they so reasoned within themselves, he said unto them, Why reason ye these things in your hearts? 9 Whether is it easier to say to the sick of the palsy, Thy sins be forgiven thee; or to say, Arise, and take up thy bed, and walk? 10 **But that ye may know that the Son of man hath power on earth to forgive sins,** (he saith to the sick of the palsy,)*

The scribes were correct in verse seven, saying that only God has the authority to forgive sins. When you and I sin, our sin is against a Holy God. It offends Him because we have transgressed His law. Let me illustrate: If Joe were to

137

punch Bob in the nose, and Pete said to Joe, "I forgive you," we would think it strange. Since Pete was not the one assaulted, the offense lies with Bob, and it is Bob who has the right to forgive, not Pete. Because Jesus is God, Jesus is offended by man's sin, and He has the right and power to forgive sin. The reason Jesus told the man sick of the palsy, "thy sins be forgiven thee," instead of telling him, "be healed" is explained for us in verse ten. Jesus was communicating that He has the power to forgive sins because He is God.

John 5:18

> *Therefore the **Jews sought the more to kill him**, because he not only had broken the sabbath, but said also that God was his Father, **making himself equal with God**.*

Jesus caused great controversy in Jerusalem when He healed a blind man by the pool of Bethesda on the Sabbath. Jesus exhibited that He was above man's law and that He had the power to heal. They understood that He meant God was his Father. He was claiming His deity, and they sought to kill Him because they thought it was blasphemous for a man to claim to be equal with God.

John 8:56-59

> *Your father Abraham rejoiced to see my day: and he saw it, and was glad. 57 Then said the Jews unto him, Thou art not yet fifty years old, and hast thou seen Abraham? 58 Jesus said*

unto them, Verily, verily, I say unto you, **Before**
Abraham was, I am. *59 Then took* **they up**
stones to cast at him: *but Jesus hid himself,*
and went out of the temple, going through the
midst of them, and so passed by.

In verse fifty-eight Jesus adopts the holy title of God as the
"I AM." Jesus was referencing to the title God identified
himself as at the burning-bush encounter (Ex 3:14). Jesus
infuriated the Jews. How can a man who is under the age of
fifty years say he has seen the patriarch Abraham? Who
does he think he is ascribing himself as the "I AM"? This
was blasphemous for a *man* to say, so the Jews tried to
stone Jesus for his blasphemy. Now, it would be blasphemous for Jesus to make these remarks if He were *just a*
man. But because He is God, it is not blasphemy.

John 10:30-33

I and my Father are one. *31 Then the Jews*
took up stones again to stone him. 32 Jesus
answered them, Many good works have I
shewed you from my Father; for which of those
works do ye stone me? 33 The Jews answered
him, saying, **For a good work we stone thee**
not; but for blasphemy; and because that
thou, being a man, makest thyself God.

This passage is perhaps the clearest of my examples. There
is no confusion here; the Jews knew exactly what Jesus was
saying. He claimed He was one in person with God the Father. You can be one with another in unity and not be the

same person. For example, we can all cry together in a rally saying "we are one," meaning that we are united in one aim, one purpose. We can be one in a union or a covenant organization, but Christ was saying something different here, and the Jews understood Him clearly. Verse thirty-three speaks for itself. Jesus claimed to be God.

Matthew 26:63-66

> *But Jesus held his peace. And the high priest answered and said unto him, I adjure thee by the living God, that thou **tell us whether thou be the Christ, the Son of God.** 64 Jesus saith unto him, Thou hast said: nevertheless I say unto you, Hereafter shall ye see the Son of man sitting on the right hand of power, and coming in the clouds of heaven. 65 Then the high priest rent his clothes, saying, **He hath spoken blasphemy;** what further need have we of witnesses? behold, **now ye have heard his blasphemy.** 66 What think ye? They answered and said, He is guilty of death.*

Jesus is now facing criminal charges for His blasphemy in Jerusalem's high court. In verse sixty-four He affirms the charge of Caiaphas, the High Priest in the previous verse. Upon hearing Christ's response Caiaphas declared there is no need to hear anymore witnesses because Jesus had witnessed against Himself by claiming a title of God.

John 20:28

*And Thomas answered and said unto him, My
Lord and my God.*

We have looked at the five times Jesus claimed to be God.
However, I think the clearest passage to prove Christ's deity is the exchange Christ had with the apostle Thomas.
Thomas was absent the first time Christ appeared to the disciples, and he said he would not believe unless he could
thrust his hand into Christ's side or put his finger into the
nail prints in His hands. However, when Christ appeared to
His disciples again, Thomas was there, and Jesus offered
His body to Thomas for inspection. Then Thomas con-
fessed that the man standing before him was not only his
Lord but also His God. This would have been a great time
for Jesus to rebuke Thomas and set him straight for his error if Jesus was *merely a man* and prophet. But Jesus did
not rebuke him. Instead Christ praised him by saying,
"You believe because you have seen; blessed are they who
believe but have not seen." (John 20:29)

REFUTING THEIR CLAIM THAT JESUS
WAS NOT CRUCIFIED

There are two verses in the Qur'an that say Jesus did not
die on a cross. They claim Allah rescued Isa (Jesus) and
took Him to heaven.

Surah 4:157-158

*"And their saying: Surely we have killed the
Messiah, Isa son of Marium, the apostle of*

*Allah; and they did not kill him nor did they crucify him, but **it appeared to them so like Isa** ......and they killed him not for sure. Nay! **Allah took him up to Himself;** ..."*

Many Muslim scholars suggest that the image of Jesus was taken off of Him and put on Judas who went to the cross to fool everyone into thinking that Jesus died on the cross. They say that the disciples either bribed or overpowered the Roman soldiers and stole the body of Judas, which they thought was Christ's, in order to make everyone believe that Christ resurrected from the grave. So let's analyze this claim.

a.   If we follow and believe this verse then we can blame Allah for Christians believing that Christ died on the cross. Allah is responsible for billions of people believing something contrary to Islam. This is a serious flaw in the Qur'an making Allah responsible for the *grand deception* that is the hallmark of the Christian faith.

b.   There is another contradiction here because there are two passages in the Qur'an that tell us Jesus died. In Surah 3:144 the Qur'an says that all the prophets before Muhammad have died. Now Jesus is not specifically mentioned in that verse, but He is included as one of the prophets who existed before Muhammad. However, in Surah 5:75 we clearly find that Jesus died.

The Messiah [Jesus], son of Mary, was only a messenger; messengers before him had indeed passed away.

Which is it? Was Jesus rescued into heaven by Allah or did He die? We have a contradiction.

c. We can turn to a number of sources that validate the Biblical record about the crucifixion. A number of secular historic records authenticate the crucifixion.

- *Josephus' Antiquities of the Jews* – Book 18,20

- *Testimonium Flavianum*

- Roman Records – *Annals of Pontius Pilate*

- Greek archeologist *Vasilius Tzaferis* (1968)

We also have the validation of the disciples' testimony and actions. Twelve times Christ made public and private appearances after His death and resurrection. Thousands had seen the resurrected Savior, and the truth of the event was so compelling that the disciples were prepared to face tortuous deaths for this truth. The burden of proof lies upon Muslims to explain why the disciples gave up their lives for a hoax.

CHAPTER SEVENTEEN

MUHAMMAD IS A FALSE PROPHET

In this chapter we make a theological case that Muhammad was a false prophet. We also make a scientific case that Muhammad was making up the revelations he claimed were coming from God. All are simple logical deductions that any open minded individual could easily grasp and accept.

THE TROUBLE WITH ABSOLUTES

The Qur'an makes a number of absolute statements about the prophet Muhammad. This creates a huge problem for Islam because, if we prove just one statement to be false, then the kingdom of Islam comes crashing down. Let me explain.

Have you ever flown off the handle in a fit of rage and said something stupid to your parents or your best friend like, "I'm *never* going to talk to you again"? The moment you speak, you lost face and proved yourself a liar. Absolutes can paint you into a corner quickly. For example, if you were to say "there is no gold in Montana", to prove your absolute statement you would have to look under every rock, search every home, business, and store in the vast

145

state of Montana for any gold. However, if you were to find a grandma in Montana, and she so happened to have one single tooth, but that tooth had a gold filling in it, your absolute statement would be proven false because gold was found in Montana.

THE PARACLETE

The Qur'an makes an absolute statement about their prophet Muhammad in Surah 7:157. It claims that the Bible foretells the coming of the prophet Muhammad.

> *Surah 7:157   Those who follow the Apostle, the <u>unlettered Prophet</u>, whom they find mentioned in their own Scriptures in the <u>Law and the Gospel</u>.*

It was easy for Muhammad to make this claim knowing that it would sound good to his followers and it would validate his apostleship, and, best of all, no one would be able to prove him wrong. Many of his followers could not read or write, and they did not have access to the Holy Scriptures. Today this verse, however, creates a problem for Muslims because they have access to the Holy Bible and they now have the burden to find the prophecy about Muhammad in the books of the Law and the books of the Gospels.

Let's break this down and look at it closely. Muhammad is called the Unlettered Prophet. It is widely contended that Muhammad could not read or write, but don't make the mistake of thinking he was dumb. He became wealthy because of his marriage to Kadijah and was able to hire a scribe Zayd ibn Thabit to read and write for him. No Muslim is going to argue that the Unlettered Prophet was not Muhammad.

The later part of the verse 157 says he is mentioned in the books of the Law (Genesis, Exodus, Leviticus, Numbers, and Deuteronomy) and the books of the Gospels (Matthew, Mark, Luke, and John). Muslims have the burden of proof that Muhammad is mentioned in these books. If they cannot prove it, then the Qur'an has an error and Muslims don't have a perfect book of scripture.

After searching the Bible, Muslims claim that the prophecy predicting the coming of Muhammad is found in Deuteronomy 18:18, in the books of the law,

> *I will raise them up a Prophet from among their brethren, like unto thee, and will put my words in his mouth; and he shall speak unto them all that I shall command him.*

The distinguishing feature of this prophet is that the words of God will be put into his mouth. Wow! That could be just about any prophet of God as every prophet will say that God has put His words in them to speak. We could say this fits Jeremiah as he found the words of God and ate them. Or perhaps King David as he hid God's word in his heart. Maybe it is Isaiah who had his lips touched with hot coals in the throne room of heaven. However, it is strongly believed that this verse is fulfilled in Jesus Christ. Jesus said in John 8:28, "then shall ye know that I am he, and that I do nothing of myself; but as my Father hath taught me, I speak these things." Also John 12:50 says, "Whatsoever I speak therefore, even as the Father said unto me, so I speak." John 17:8 says, "For I have given unto them the words which thou gavest me."

The passage in the Law is somewhat ambiguous, so let's turn to the passage in the Gospels. This is where we come to the *Paraclete*. This is not an ambiguous term because only one person can be the *Paraclete*. Muslim scholars have chosen the passage in John 16:7. Jesus is speaking here:

> *Nevertheless I tell you the truth; It is expedient for you that I go away: for if I go not away, the Comforter will not come unto you; but if I depart, I will send him unto you.*

John 15:26 also supports this idea.

> *But when the Comforter is come, whom I will send unto you from the Father, even the Spirit of truth, which proceedeth from the Father, he shall testify of me:*

Muslims proclaim that the Comforter, which in the Greek is *Paraclete,* is none other than Muhammad. Jesus declared that He must depart so that the *Paraclete* can arrive. The idea is Jesus needs to finish his task quickly so that the Paraclete can come to do his work. Muhammad arrived six hundred years after Christ, so we can't say Jesus had to leave in order for Muhammad to show up. Also, Muslims are very dogmatic that God is not a father, but the Comforter is going to come from the Father. This does not go well with Islamic theology.

The paramount problem for Muslims is that the Bible clearly teaches us who the *Paraclete* is in John 14:26, "But the Comforter [is] the Holy Ghost, whom the Father will send in [Christ's] name". Here we have it; the *Paraclete* is the Holy Ghost. Islam recognizes the Holy Spirit as a working force who enables the power of God, so they would not attribute Muhammad as being the Holy Spirit, this would spell trouble for Islam. We know that Deuteronomy 18:18 could be any prophet, and most likely it is Christ. We also know that the *Paraclete* is not Muhammad in the Gospels. The Qur'an made an absolute statement that doesn't cut the mustard. This attests to the fact that Muhammad was a con artist.

SATANIC VERSES

Muslims try to claim Deuteronomy 18:18 to be their prophet. Ironically a serious warning is given to false prophets just two verses away in Deuteronomy 18:20-22.

> *But the prophet, which shall presume to speak a word in my name, which I have not commanded him to speak, or that shall speak in the name of other gods, even <u>that prophet shall die</u>. 21 And if thou say in thine heart, How shall we know the word which the LORD hath not spoken? 22 When a prophet speaketh in*

> *the name of the LORD, <u>if the thing follow not,</u>*
> <u>*nor come to pass,*</u> *that is the thing which the*
> *LORD hath not spoken, but the prophet hath*
> *spoken it presumptuously: thou shalt not be*
> *afraid of him.*

The consequence for impersonating a prophet of God carries the death penalty. The standard was strict; the prophet of God had to be completely accurate all of the time, and if his predictions did not come to pass, it showed that he was not God's man, he was not to be feared, and he was to be killed.

Perhaps you may have heard of the *Satanic Verses.* They are found in chapter 53:19-20 in the Qur'an,

> *Have ye thought upon al-Lat and al-Uzza And*
> *Manat, the third, the other?*

Muhammad preached monotheism to his followers saying there is only one God, Allah. However, Muhammad experienced great resistance from his tribal peers, the Qurayish. They worshiped multiple gods, and it seems there was an attempt to accommodate the polytheists a little by adding this verse about three female deities, al-Lat, al-Uzza and Manat who were popular deities amongst the Qurayish tribe in Mecca. The Qurayish believed that star goddess al-Lat was the mother of Allah the moon god, and his daughters were the stars al-Uzza and Manat.

These verses in the Qur'an were given in an attempt to appease the Qurayish polytheists but it angered Muhammad's followers. They were indignant that Muhammad would accommodate the polytheists with these goddesses. After all, now they were to be monotheist. Muhammad was between a rock and a hard place, so his remedy was to proclaim that the devil made him do it. He claimed that an elevated crane (the devil) tricked him to recite these verses. These traditions are from two hadiths: Dar al-Fikr ed. vol. 3 p. 293 and Dar Sadir, vol. 1 p. 205. This is also well documented by the Muslim British author Salmon Rushdie who still lives in hiding with a fatwa on his head for exposing this dirty secret of Islam in the book *Satanic Verses.*

This raises the question, "How can a prophet of God confuse Satanic revelations with his angel messenger, Gabriel?" If he is truly a prophet of God, he is to be completely accurate all of the time. Yet we have another reason to claim Muhammad was a con man, a fake, a deceiver.

LIST OF ERRORS AND CONTRADICTIONS

Islam wants us to believe Allah is the author of the Holy Bible, yet the Qur'an is very unlike the Holy Bible. The Bible is harmoniously written by forty different men over a period of two thousand years, yet it bears no contradictions. The Qur'an, comes from one prophet over a period of twenty years and is full of errors and contradictions. I want to credit my friend Sam Shamoun for many entries in the following list:

- Surah 19:23-36 says Jesus is born under a palm tree.

- Surah 19:27-28 says the mother of Jesus is Maryum the sister of Aaron (and Moses).

- Surah 7:157 has Moses praying to God and referencing a verse in the Gospels which was written one thousand years after Moses lived.

- Adam was created from the dust of the ground in Surah 3:59, but in Surahs 19:67 and 52:35, Adam is created from nothing. In Surah 96:2, Adam was created from congealed blood. In in Surah 16:4, he is made from a drop of sperm.

- All of Noah's sons were saved from the flood in Surahs 21:76 and 37:77, but in Surah 11:42-43, one son drowns in the flood.

- Who is the first Muslim? In Surah 39:12, Muhammad said he was. Surah 7:143 says it was Moses. Surah 2:132 says it was Abraham.

- Pharaoh's magicians believed in God in Surahs 7:103-126, 20:56-73, and 26:29-51, but in Surah 10:83 *only* the Israelites believed in God.

- Pharaoh lives through the Red Sea incident in Surah 10:90-92, but in Surah 17:102-103, he drowns in the Red Sea.

- Surah's 9:17 and 9:69 clearly state that Allah will not reward the good deeds of the *Kufr*. Yet Surahs 99:7 and 2:62 say the Kufr (Unbelievers) will be rewarded. Also Surahs 9:28-33, 5:17, and 72-73 call

Christians idolaters, and Surah 9:17 is clear that idolaters will not be rewarded.

- Surahs 22:47 and 32:5 say a day with God is one thousand years, but in Surah 70:4 it is fifty thousand years.

- Surah 7:149 has Aaron and the Jews repenting from their worship of the golden calf before Moses returns, but in Surah 20:91, they refuse to repent.

- In the Judgement, Surah 56:7 says there will be three groups present, but in Surahs 90:18-19 and 99:6-8, there are only two present.

- Surah 54:19 says it took Allah one day to destroy the people of Aad, but in Surahs 41:16 and 69:6-7, it took several days.

- Surah 4:48, 116 say that Allah does not forgive Shirk, but Surahs 4:153, 25:68-71 shows Allah forgiving Shirk.

- Surah 5:69 says Christians have nothing to fear on the last day, but three verses later, in Surah 5:72, Christians are going to hell.

- The story of Lot in Surah's 7:82 and 27:56 conflict with the account in Surah 29:29.

- In Surah 16:49-50, all angels obey God, but in Surah 2:34, we see that they can disobey God.

- In Surah 35:1, angels can have as many as six wings, but Muhammad said Gabriel had six hundred wings. Sahih al-Bukhari Vol 4; Book54; Page455

EMPIRICAL SCIENTIFIC PROBLEMS

Unlike the Holy Bible, the Qur'an fails with empirical science. Science has a way of catching up with the Holy Bible. Centuries ago scientists believed the world was flat, but the Bible said that Earth was a circle in Isaiah 40:22. Medical doctors used to bleed patients in order to cure disease, but the Scriptures told us that life was in the blood in Leviticus 17:11. Furthermore, scientists recently discovered that there are fresh water springs in the seas and oceans, just as the earliest book of the Bible revealed in Job 38:16.

Here's an example of how Islam can be proven false with empirical science:

> *Surah 18:83-86 - They ask thee concerning Zul-qarnain. ....and We gave him the ways and the means to all ends. ...when he reached the setting of **the sun, he found it set in a spring of murky water:** Near it he found a People:*

We know Zul-Qarain better as Alexander the Great. According to Muhammad, this great Greek conqueror was aided in his conquests by Allah, who one day brought him to the edge of the earth to see where the sun sets. He found people living near the edge of the earth and witnessed the sun setting into water. In Muhammad's day, it was still believed that the earth was flat and these traditions were ex-

154

pressed in his reciting. To believe in Islam is to believe that the earth is flat, which we now know to be folklore.

CHAPTER EIGHTEEN

THE SINKING QUR'AN

Islam is defeated if the Qur'an cannot stand the same tests that the Holy Bible has been put through. For hundreds of years, critics of the Bible have been attempting to destroy it, but each test they put it under, the Holy Bible comes up smelling like a rose. Muslims are not permitted to question their faith; they are commanded to believe even if the evidence is thin. Therefore, the Qur'an has had little scrutiny until recently. As Islam is moving into our colleges in the West, professors are asking Muslim scholars to back up their claims about having a superior religion and a perfect, un-adulterated scripture. Muslims have been very reluctant to let the textual critics examine their ancient manuscripts, but now that we have, we find that the history of the Qur'an is full of holes and is sinking to a watery grave.

To explain this point well, I first need to explain what Muslims now believe to be true about their Qur'an.

1. Muhammad never commanded for the Qur'an to be written. It was to be kept in their hearts by memorizing and reciting it. Those who memorize the Qur'an were called *Qurra* meaning reciters. Sometimes they are referred to as a *Hafiz* meaning a Guardian of the Qur'an. Early on, various versions

and renderings began to develop which, caused no small controversy among the Muslims. Read the testimony from Ka'b, an early convert of Muhammad and one who memorized the Qur'an, a Hafiz.

"Ubayy b. Ka'b reported: I was in the mosque when a man entered and prayed and recited the Qur'an in a style to which I objected. Then another man entered the mosque and recited in a style different from that of his companion. When we had finished the prayer, we all went to Allah's Messenger and said to him: This man recited in a style to which I objected, and the other entered and recited in a style different from that of his companion. The Messenger of Allah asked them to recite and so they recited, and the Apostle of Allah expressed approval of their affairs their modes of recitation. And there occurred in my mind a sort of denial which did not occur even during the Days of Ignorance. When the Messenger of Allah saw how I was affected by a wrong idea, he struck my chest, whereupon I broke into sweating and felt as though I were looking at Allah with fear. He said to me: Ubayy, a message was sent to me to recite the Qur'an in one dialect, and I replied: Make things easy for my people. It was conveyed to me for the second time that it should be recited in two dialects. I again replied to him: Make affairs easy for my people. It was again conveyed to me for the third time to recite in seven dialects...."

Sahih Muslim 4,1787

2. We find some attempted to collect the Surahs of the Qur'an, but most of them were written in fragments. Neither of the first two Caliphs were eager to commission a writing of the Qur'an because they were afraid to "do something which Allah's apostle has not done" (Sahih Bukhari 6;60;201).

3. However, during Uthman's reign, about twenty years after Muhammad's death, a great number of Qurra's were killed in the battle of *Yamama* and they feared they might lose the Qur'an. Uthman then ordered a perfect Qur'an to be written, and he made copies to send throughout the realm. Reportedly, four copies were made.

4. Uthman picked four people for the task and gave them instructions of how they were to perform the task.

"Uthman then ordered Zaid bin Thabit, 'Abdullah bin AzZubair, Said bin Al-As and 'AbdurRahman bin Harith bin Hisham to rewrite the manuscripts in perfect copies. 'Uthman said to the three Quraishi men, "In case you disagree with Zaid bin Thabit on any point in the Qur'an, then write it in the dialect of Quraish, the Qur'an was revealed in their tongue."... 'Uthman sent to every Muslim province one copy of what they had copied, and ordered that all the other Qur'anic materials, whether written in fragmentary manuscripts or whole copies, be burnt. Said bin Thabit added, "A Verse

from Surat Ahzab was missed by me when
we copied the Qur'an and I used to hear
Allah's Apostle reciting it. So we searched
for it and found it with Khuzaima bin Thabit
Al-Ansari. (That Verse was): 'Among the
Believers are men who have been true in
their covenant with Allah."

Sahih Bukhari 6:61:510

So far, we have only dealt with the original Qur'an and are already finding many problems. We have not even cut into the many variants of the succeeding manuscripts.

I hope you are understanding the importance of the above evidence. The Islamic historic record tells us that the task of writing the Qur'an was given to four fallible men who were left to use human discernment in determining what verses belonged and did not belong. The fall back method that they were to use if they could not agree was to use the dialect of the Qurayish. So there was guess work going on here. When they completed their work, it was discovered that they left out a verse. I am thankful that as Christians our Bible does not have this trouble in its history.

Muslims need to answer these arguments:

(1)   Muslims suggest the Prophet who receives the revelation is acting under Holy inspiration. They do not claim the person who writes it down or recites it is doing so under the power of Holy inspiration. So how can

159

we be assured that the four writers picked the right verses or the right dialects to be in the perfect Qur'an? After all, we had a twenty-year gap between Muhammad and Uthman's Qur'an.

(2)   If it were suggested that the four were working with the enabling of supernatural inspiration, why would they need rules to handle disagreements?

(3)   The testimony shows that the four needed the help of other manuscripts to create their perfect Qur'an. Why was it necessary to burn the manuscripts that were used to make their perfect Qur'an? Was there something to hide?

(4)   Also, how do we reconcile the fact that after their work was completed and copies were made, they discovered that they left something out? If they made the mistake of leaving something out, they could have added something that should not be there.

(5)   If the perfect Qur'an had a missing verse, is it perfect? It seems to me something cannot be improved if it is perfect.

We face nothing like this when dealing with the manuscripts of the Holy Bible. So far, it is fair to say that the Qur'an is in trouble, but it is going to go from bad to worse. We have only just started to reveal the holes in the story of the Qur'an.

EXAMINING THE EXTANT MANUSCRIPTS OF THE QUR'AN

Earlier we learned that there were four Uthman (perfect) Qur'ans. These are the originals, and Muslims have been telling us that two of them are still around to this day. Now that they are allowing people in the West to examine them, they are finding a world of trouble.

It is important we understand how scholars date manuscripts. One form of dating is using the radiocarbon dating method. When an organic substance dies it loses carbon over a period of years in the process of decay. Current carbon levels can imply the age of the substance. This method assumes a constant rate of carbon radiation, so it is not reliable. It has given rise to some excitement about an ancient manuscript found recently in the dusty archives of the University of Birmingham in England.[39] Carbon dating is suggesting that the Qur'an predates Muhammad himself. Here is the problem about this dating method. The vellum or papyrus may be older than Muhammad. The ink may be older too. But it does not tell us the date the words were penned. For example, today, I may inscribe a letter on paper that was milled during the American Revolution and use ink from an ink well that that came off the Mayflower. Carbon dating cannot indicate when I penned my letter.

The more reliable method of dating is studying the style of script being used. Languages are always going through developments: alphabet, spelling, idioms, colloquialisms, etc. The Arabic alphabet was very much in its infancy during Muhammad's day. The first real book published in Arabia was the Qur'an. The Arabic language was like the Hebrew language in that it was a consonantal language. There were no vowels in their alphabet in Muhammad's days. Vowels did not appear until about one hundred to one hundred fifty years after Muhammad. We should expect these early Qur'ans were written in what is known as a Nabataean script, which had no diacritical marks or vowels.

The two oldest manuscripts that are extant and widely purported to be the perfect Uthman Qur'ans are the Samarquand and the Topkapi manuscripts.[40] The Samarquand is located in Hast Imam library, in Tashkent, Uzbekistan[41] and is in the control of the Russians. The other manuscript is kept in the Topkapi Palace Museum, Istanbul, Turkey.[42] The Topkapi manuscript is more complete than the Samarquand as it is only missing a couple of leaves. The Samarquand, on the other hand, has many parts missing.[43]

Here is the bombshell: neither of them are written in a Nabataean script. Rather, they are written in the Kufic script which was developed at least one hundred fifty years after Muhammad. The Kufic script has diacritical marks which show the vowels in Arabic.

Furthermore, all of the Sunah is from one hundred to one hundred fifty years after Muhammad. The Sirat and the

Hadiths, are not the records from the companions of Muhammad themselves but rather the children and grand-children of companions of Muhammad. A logical thinking person could be forgiven to think that there is opportunity for embellishments and additions of imaginations to slip into the Islamic record.

Guilty of Plagiarism

I want to credit my friend Jay Smith in London for his studious work here. There are numerous stories that are contained in the Qur'an that follow the legends of stories written many years before Muhammad very closely.

1. Muhammad's Night Journey

Surah 17 describes a literal bodily journey by night upon the back of a fabulous steed, not merely to the further temple (the temple of Jerusalem), but to heaven itself, where the Prophet ascended from story to story until he reached the very presence of God and learned many of the secrets of heaven. This story comes from a Persian myth found in the "Arta' Viraf Namak" which was written some four hundred years before his time.

2. Solomon's Bird Air Force

One beloved story is from the Second Targum of Ester, which dates to the second century; Targums were fictional stories using Bible characters to teach moral lessons for children. This story is plagiarized in Surah 27:17-44.

King Solomon had birds trained to pick up rocks and drop them on the enemy. I guess this is the first air force. One day the hoopoe bird was missing from his duties. Solomon finds him and learns the hoopoe bird was off to visit the Queen of Sheba. The hoopoe bird brags about the greatness of Solomon and his kingdom and invites her to come to meet Solomon. A funny part of the story is that, when she comes to the throne room, there is a mirrored floor that she thinks is water so she lifts her skirt to keep it dry. The part of the story that is in the Targum but not in the Qur'an is that when she lifted up her skirt it revealed that her legs were very hairy.

3. More stories that found their way into the Qur'an:

    a. The Story of Cain and the Raven in Surah 5:31-34 comes from three sources: a. Targum of Joziah (200 AD), b. Targum of Jerusalem, and c. Pirke De Rabbi Eliezer (100 BC)

    b. The Story of Abraham destroying smaller idols with a larger idol in Surah 21:51-71 is found in the Midrash Genesis Rabbah, which was five hundred years before Muhammad.

    c. The story of Jesus born under a palm tree in Surah 19:29-33 comes from an Apocryphal Gospel, which was three hundred years before Muhammad.

d. The story of Jesus making birds out of clay in Surah 3:49 is from the Gospel of Thomas which was five hundred years before Muhammad.

Muhammad claimed that his source for the Qur'an was the Angel Gabriel. Well, the evidence is in; Muhammad borrowed from the Bible and many other sources to make up his scriptures.

The Noble Qur'an is not so noble after all. Many say that the Devil wrote it. I have read it many times now and believe me, if the Devil wrote it, it would be better written. About one fifth of the book in-comprehensible. Muslims call this the mystery of Allah. It's a mystery to me why anyone would dare claim this book to be superior to the Holy Bible. There is no time element to the Qur'an. One can get a time concept if they overlay the life of Muhammad to the Qur'an but then it is still lacking a narrative. The only narrative that can be found in it, is when the Qur'an tells stories that Muhammad thought were in the Holy Bible.

I would not credit the Devil with the authorship of the Qur'an, but I don't want you to think that he did not influence Muhammad in the content of the Qur'an. Remember, Muhammad claims that the *recitings,* that we call the Qur'an, were given to him by the Jinn who they believed to be the Angel Gabriel. In this book we have already established that this Jinn was not a spirit from heaven but rather a spirit from the Devil, a demon. In short, the Qur'an was influenced by the Devil, but the construction of the Qur'an is a poor man-made work of fiction.

CHAPTER NINETEEN

HOW DOES IT END

1Peter 4:17 For the time is come that judgment must begin at the house of God: and if it first begin at us, what shall the end be of them that obey not the gospel of God?

I believe I have made a convincing case to prove that Muhammad was a clever con artist rather than a prophet of God. He used his god Allah as a sock puppet to inspire men to fight battles gaining him much wealth, fame, sex and power. He established ideologies that masquerade as a religion, and sadly, those who bought into it will face an eternity in Hell.

The Bible warns that we all have an appointment with death and after that there is a judgment (Hebrews 9:27). There are two judgements, one for the saved and one for the lost. The Judgment Seat of Christ (2 Corinthians 5:10) is where the saved will be judged, not to see if we as Christians are going to heaven, but we will be judged for our works. Christians won't lose their place in heaven, but will lose some of the rewards God wanted to bestow upon them.

That Judgment will take place during the seven year tribulation period on Earth. I want to draw your attention to the next judgment, the Great White Throne Judgment found in

Revelation 20:11-15. All the souls of earth from the beginning of time to the end will be present. The Saints will be there to observe all those throughout history who have rejected Christ's gift of salvation. Let me remind you, there are 1.8 billion Muslims today. They, along with all the Muslims of these past fourteen hundred years, will also be judged. Perhaps three to four billion souls will be there because they followed the lies of Muhammad. They were deceived into believing that Jesus was just a man and that Christianity was false. They were swindled by a trickster, a deceiver. Perhaps before they take the stand themselves, they might all observe Muhammad receiving his judgment first.

The Bible tells us what is going to happen at this judgment in Philippians 2:10-11,

> *"That at the name of Jesus every knee should bow, of things in heaven, and things in earth, and things under the earth; 11 And that every tongue should confess that Jesus Christ is Lord, to the glory of God the Father.*

Every Muslim who bent the knee to Allah will see their prophet Muhammad bend his knee to the Almighty, Jesus Christ. Muhammad will confess with his own lips that Jesus Christ is the LORD. Then they will witness the angels of heaven throw Muhammad into the Lake of Fire where he will remain for all eternity. The same tragic fate will befall every Muslim who followed Muhammad and any others who have rejected Christ's gift of salvation.

I hope this breaks your heart because God does not rejoice in bringing punishment to the wicked (Ezekiel 18:32). Proverbs 24:17 prohibits rejoicing when our enemy falls or stumbles.

To close, I wish to encourage you with this thought. God is sovereign, and His blessing on our nation can continue if we seek after Him and return to His paths of righteousness. God brought judgment many times on Israel in the Old Testament for their disobedience. He would raise up calamities and many times an enemy because the people rejected the warnings of the prophets and did not repent. When the pain became too unbearable, the Jews would finally repent and return back to God. God would forgive and restore them to blessing, and He would turn His hand on those who were against Israel. I sincerely believe that there is still hope for America if we repent. I believe God is using Islam as an instrument of judgment and it is my prayer that we will, like Israel did, repent and return.

I think it is prudent to close with the verse that gives us God's roadmap to revival. If nations get off the path, here is how they return:

II Chronicles 7:14

If my people, which are called by my name, shall humble themselves, and pray, and seek my face, and turn from their wicked ways; then will I hear from heaven, and will forgive their sin, and will heal their land.

We think we are the ones in the waiting room waiting on God to open the windows of Heaven and drop revival down on us.

But NO! It is God who is in the waiting room waiting on us to do four things. Humble ourselves, pray, seek God's face and turn from our wicked ways. When we get busy doing our part, then we allow God to do his part which is at the end of verse fourteen. He will forgive our sin and heal our land.

God has given us a roadmap to revival and a recipe for national repentance. Revival can only come through the door of repentance. The heart is cold, dark, indifferent and hardened with sin. We cannot push the silken thread of revival into a hardened heart. There must be a sharp needle of repentance to pierce through the heart, and pull the thread of revival through it.

America, repent and turn back to God. Christians, stand and oppose the evil teaching of Islam. Expose it, speak the truth in love. Be courageous. Have compassion on the Muslim and seek to rescue them and guide them into the light of the Gospel.

GLOSSARY OF TERMS

Term	Sounds Like	Brief Definition
Allah Akhbar	ah-lah ock-bar	god (Allah) is greatest or greater
Al-sabi	owl-sa-bee	Capture of women to be made concubines or sex slaves for warriors.
As-salamu alaykum	a-sa-lom alay-cum	The traditional Muslim greeting – Peace be upon you.
Ayat	eye-ya	A verse in the Qur'an
Bismallah	biz-ma-luh	A blessing that Precedes every chapter (surah) in the Qur'an. "In the name of Allah, the most Gracious, the most Merciful."
Caliph	kal-ef	Successor of Muhammad. The Emperor of the Empire or Ummah
Caliphate	kal-e-fait	Dictatorship over the Ummah
Dajjal	da-jaw	The Anti-Christ – Liar – Deceiver
Dar a Harb	dar–al–harb	House of War or Infidel
Dar a Islam	dar-al-Is-lom	House of Submission
Da'wah	da-wuh	Proselytizing – Evangelism
Dhimmi	de-me	2nd Class. Technically, the "protected one"

171

Tom Wallace Jr.

Term	Sounds Like	Brief Definition
EID al Ftir	eed-a-fit-ur	Feast - Celebrating the end of Ramadan.
EID al Adha	eed-a-aduh	Feast – Celebrating Abraham's faith to sacrifice his son Ishmael
Fatwa	fot-wah	A legal binding opinion from an Islamic scholar
Fiqh	fik	Legal Jurisprudence in Shariah law
Hadith	ha-deeth	Traditions of Mohammad Things his companions saw the prophet say or do.
Hafiz	Ha-fez	Guardian of the recitings (Qur'an)
Hajj	hawj	Pillar of Islam - Pilgrimage to Mecca
Halal	ha-lowl	Permitted or Approved (food)
Haram	hh-rom	Forbidden
Hijab	hh-jab	Head covering like a scarf but does not veil the face.
Imam	e-mom	Mosque leader (preacher / teacher)
Injil	in-jeel	The four Gospels
Isa	e-sa	The Muslim Jesus
Jihad	jee-hod	Struggle against evil the Kufar (Legal definition is War to establish Islam)
Jinn	jin	Spirit. Demon or an Angel.

Term	Sounds Like	Brief Definition
Jizya	jis-yuh	Protection tax or Poll tax. Extorted from Non-Muslims.
Ka'aba	kaw-bah	Cube shape Temple in Mecca
Kafr	ka-fur	Vile word for unbeliever. The filth or excrement. The word used in the Qur'an to describe the infidel, the unbeliever.
Khums	Cooms	Tax. Literally a fifth. War booty tax
Kufr	coo-far	Singlur of Kafr.
Madhhab	mud-hob	Type of doctrine of Islamic law. School of thought or interpretation.
Madrasah	ma-dras-uh	School
Mahdi	ma-h-dee	Messiah – 'a guide'
Mecca	meh-ka	Holiest city in Islam. The birth place of Muhammad.
Medina	ma-dee-nuh	City of the prophets. About 100km North of Mecca in Arabia
Minaret	meen-a-ret	Prayer tower at a mosque.
Mufti	muf-tee	Scholar who can issue Fatwas.
Mullah	mu-la	Scholar of the Qur'an,Hadith & Fiqh
Muslim	moos-lim	The surrendered one

Tom Wallace Jr.

Term	Sounds Like	Brief Definition
P.B.U.H.		means Peace Be Upon Him
Qibla	Kib-luh	Direction of prayers
Qu'ran or Koran	ko-ran or k'ran	The recitations of Allah given to the prophet through the Angel Gabriel.
Qurra	ko-ruh	The reciters. Sometimes called Hafiz
Ramadhan	rom-a-don	Month of fasting. Eating only permitted after Sunset.
Sahih	Sa-hee	Approved, genuine, authentic.
Salam	sa-lom	Peace
Salat	sa-lat	Pillar of Islam - Prayer
S.A.W.S		*Sallallahu Alayhi Wa Sallam* - Arabic for PBUH
Sawm	sowm	Pillar of Islam - Fasting
Shahadah	shh-ha-da	Pillar of Islam – The Muslim Creed "There is no God but Allah and Muhammad is his Prophet."
Shariah	sha-ree-a	Literally 'the pathway' - Islamic law
Shaykh or Sheik	shake	Spiritual master – ruler
Shi'ite or Shia	she-ite or she-a	2nd largest sect in Islam – about 12%. Believes the caliph should be a blood line of the prophet Muhammad.

Term	Sounds Like	Brief Definition
Shirk	sherk	Greatest sin – blasphemy. Making something or someone equal to God.
Sirat or **Sira**	seer-uh	The Biography (of Mohammad) written by Ibn Isaaq. Part of the Sunnah
Sunnah	soon-uh	Words of Mohammad. Combination of the Sira and the Hadith
Sunni	soon-e	Largest sect in Islam – about 80%. Believes the caliph does not have to the blood line of the prophet Muhammad.
Surah	sue-ruh	Chapter. Like Surah 9 is Chapter 9.
Taqiyya	ta-key-uh	The Doctrine of Deception. Used to confound the Kufar
Tawrat	tah-ra(t)	Scripture - The Torah or the Pentateuch. The 5 books of Moses.
Ummah	oo-muh	The Nation of Islam – the global community
Zabur	za-bore	Scripture – The holy book of David (Dawud) and Solomon. Proverbs and Psalms.
Zakat	za-kuh	Pillar of Islam - The Muslim tax – tithing.
Zoroastrian	Zor-ras-trian	Followers of Zoroaster. A cult mentioned in the OT. Many still live in Persia.

END NOTES

1 - Online Transcript by Michael S. Smith II, published 14 May, 2015. "Transcript: Al-Baghdadi's latest message" - http://insidethejihad.com/2015/05/transcript-al-baghdadis-latest-message/

2 - Found in Three Hadiths: Al-Hasan narrated by al-Tirmidhi; and al-Sunan narrated by Ibn Maahah; and by Sa'eed ibn Mansoor; and al-Kabeer narrated by al-Tabaraani.

3 - Sahih Bukhari: Vol. 1:28, 301; Vol. 2:161; Vol. 7:124-126; http://www.answering-islam.org/Women/in-hell.html

4 - Newsweek Online Magazine by Polly Mosendez published July 6, 2015 "President Obama: 'We Will Never Be at War With Islam'" - http://www.newsweek.com/watch-president-obama-speaks-pentagon-about-isis-350625

5 - Washington Post by Cheryl K. Chumley published Feb. 17, 2015 "State Department on Islamic State: We can't win 'by killing them' — need to get them jobs" http://www.washingtontimes.com/news/2015/feb/17/marie-harf-state-department-on-islamic-state-cant-/

6 - White House Transcripts – Office of the Press Secretary, "Remarks by the President at the United States Coast Guard Academy Commencement" published May 20, 2015

7 - The Sunday Times by Abul Taher, published Sept. 14, 2008 – "Revealed: UK's first official sharia courts " Front page

8 - The Daily Mail by Steve Doughty "Britain has 85 sharia courts: The astonishing spread of the Islamic justice behind closed doors" published June 29, 2009 - http://www.dailymail.co.uk/news/article-1196165/Britain-85-sharia-courts-The-astonishing-spread-Islamic-justice-closed-doors.html

9 - The Guardian by Riazat Butt "Archbishop backs sharia law for British Muslims" published Feb. 7, 2008 http://www.theguardian.com/uk/2008/feb/07/religion.world

10 - The American Thinker by Eileen F. Toplansky "The Continuing Brutal Legacy of the Religion of Peace" published Aug. 11, 2013 http://www.americanthinker.com/articles/2013/08/the_continuing_bru tal_legacy_of_the_religion_of_peace.html

11 - Fox News – The Kelly File special: The Lone Wolf published July 17, 2015

12 - PDF copy published online by the Investigative Project. http://www.investigativeproject.org/documents/misc/20.pdf

13 - Alliance Defending Freedom "Pulpit Freedom Sunday" http://www.adflegal.org/issues/religious-freedom/church/key-issues/pulpit-freedom-sunday

14 - Charles Finney Archive website. http://www.charlesgfinney.com/1868_75Independent/731204_conscie nce.htm

15 - CNW [Canadian News Wire] "Human Rights Complaints Launched Against Maclean's Magazine" published Dec. 4, 2007 - http://archive.newswire.ca/en/story/170609/human-rights-complaints-launched-against-maclean-s-magazine

16 - About page of the OIC – http://www.oicun.org/2/23/

17 - The Washington Review "Will Istanbul Process Relieve the Tension Between the Muslim World and the West?" by Turan Kayaoglu & Marie Juul Petersen, published October 2013 http://www.thewashingtonreview.org/articles/will-istanbul-process-relieve-the-tension-between-the-muslim-world-and-the-west.html

18 - State Department Transcript "Istanbul Process for Combating Intolerance and Discrimination Based on Religion or Belief" by Secretary of State Hillary Rodham Clinton delivered in Washington DC, Dec. 14, 2011. http://www.state.gov/secretary/20092013clinton/rm/2011/12/178866. htm

19 - Organization of Islamic Cooperation website News "OIC to hold the next event of the 'Istanbul Process' on combating intolerance in Geneva." Published Feb 2, 2013. http://www.oic-oci.org/oicv2/topic/?t_id=7758&ref=3157&lan=en&x_key=resolution %2016/18

20 - Belfast Telegraph by Adrian Rutherford "Pastor James McConnell solicitor argues preacher 'did not incite hatred or encourage violence against Muslims'" published June 8, 2015 - http://www.belfasttelegraph.co.uk/news/northern-ireland/pastor-james-mcconnell-solicitor-argues-preacher-did-not-incite-hatred-or-encourage-violence-against-muslims-31431784.html

21 - Maryland Constitution last ratified Nov. 6, 2012; http://msa.maryland.gov/msa/mdmanual/43const/html/00dec.html

22 - White House Transcripts by the office Press Secretary, Cairo, Egypt released June 4, 2009

23 - Middle East Media Research Institute (MEMRI) with the Jihad & Terrorism Threat Monitor (JTTM) "ISIS Issues Dhimma Contract For Christians To Sign, Orders Them To Pay Jizyah" published September 3, 2015

24 - Original source is the Persian historian, Tabari (838-923of the Hegire=310). A scholarly report on the pact of Umar is found on Al-Bushra.org - http://www.al-bushra.org/holyland/chapeter2c.htm

25 - Newsweek Magazine by Stav Ziv "Two Saudi Women Arrested for Defying Driving Ban to Be Sent to Terror Court" published Dec. 29, 2014 - http://www.newsweek.com/saudi-women-arrested-driving-be-sent-terror-court-295611

26 - The Week – "Eleven things women in Saudi Arabia cannot do" published Aug. 19, 2015 - http://www.theweek.co.uk/60339/eleven-things-women-in-saudi-arabia-cannot-do

27 - The 14 year old Malala Yousafzai brought worldwide attention to the abuse of women in the Islamic state of Pakistan. She defied the

ban on education and was shot by the Taliban. Her survival and campaign for women's rights has won her the honor of being the youngest person to win the Nobel peace prize. BBC profile her at - http://www.bbc.com/news/world-asia-23241937

28 - The Independent by Andy McSmith "Girls escape forced marriage by concealing spoons in clothing to set off metal detectors at the airport" published Aug. 15, 2013 - http://www.independent.co.uk/news/uk/crime/girls-escape-forced-marriage-by-concealing-spoons-in-clothing-to-set-off-metal-detectors-at-the-airport-8764404.html

29 - PDF   download   - https://www.gov.uk/government/uploads/system/uploads/attachment_data/file/380125/MultiAgencyPracticeGuidelinesNov14.pdf

30 - Unicif.org "TUNISIA -MENA Gender Equality Profile Status of Girls and Women in the Middle East and North Africa" published Oct, 2011 and "Oman -MENA Gender Equality Profile Status of Girls and Women in the Middle East and North Africa" published Oct, 2011. Page 1 point 2 – Legal Framework.

31 - Washington Times By Jessica Chasmar "8-year-old Yemeni girl dies from injuries sustained on her wedding night: report" published Sep. 10, 2013 - http://www.washingtontimes.com/news/2013/sep/10/8-year-old-yemeni-girl-dies-injuries-sustained-her/

32 - WND by F. Michael Maloof "Saudi religious leader Oks rape of children" published Jan 2, 2015 - http://www.wnd.com/2015/01/saudi-religious-leader-oks-rape-of-children/

33 - Unicef PDF download - http://www.unicef.org/sowc09/docs/SOWC09-CountryExample-Mali.pdf

34 - Indepdendent by Ishaan Tharoor "Isis burns woman alive for refusing to engage in 'extreme' sex act, UN says" Published Sunday

24 May 2015 - http://www.independent.co.uk/news/world/middle-east/isis-burns-woman-alive-for-refusing-to-engage-in-extreme-sex-act-un-says-10272832.html

35 - National Geographic News "Kayaking to Timbuktu, Writer Sees Slave Trade, More" by Brian Handwerk published December 5, 2002; http://news.nationalgeographic.com/news/2002/12/1206_021205_sala kkayak.html

36 - BBC World News "Mauritania country profile" published May 27, 2015; http://www.bbc.com/news/world-africa-13881985

37 - Jihad Watch by Robert Spencer "Qaradawi: "If they had gotten rid of the apostasy punishment Islam wouldn't exist today" published Feb 6, 2013 - http://www.jihadwatch.org/2013/02/qaradawi-if-they-had-gotten-rid-of-the-apostasy-punishment-islam-wouldnt-exist-today

38 - Protest Over Cartoons of Muhammad turn Deadly by Carlotta Gall, published Feb 6, 2016; http://www.nytimes.com/2006/02/06/international/middleeast/06cnd-cartoon.html

39 - Huff Post by Paul Vale "Fragments Of Ancient Quran Could Be Older Than Muhammad" posted Sep 2, 2015 – http://www.huffingtonpost.com/entry/fragments-of-ancient-quran-could-be-older-than-muhammad_55e5d58ae4b0c818f61937ce

40 - Islam Awareness "The "Qur'ān Of 'Uthmān" At The Topkapi Museum" - http://www.islamic-awareness.org/Quran/Text/Mss/topkapi.html

41 - BBC news by Ian MacWilliam "Tashkent's hidden Islamic relic" published Jan 5, 2006 - http://news.bbc.co.uk/2/hi/asia-pacific/4581684.stm

42 - Debate.org.uk "The Qur'an's Manuscript Evidence" - http://www.debate.org.uk/debate-topics/historical/the-bible-and-the-quran/the-qurans-manuscript-evidence/

43 - Islamic Awareness "The Qur'anic Manuscripts" - http://www.islamic-awareness.org/Quran/Text/Mss/